The Ultimate Entrepreneurial Success Strategy

How the Top 0.1% Generate Wealth, Prosperity, and Freedom

The 4 Pillars of Mastery

Pillar 1: Develop The Owner, Not the Business

CHRISTIAN SIMPSON

First Edition

First Edition published 2019.

Website: christian-simpson.com
Email: author@christian-simpson.com
Publisher: Christian Simpson Enterprises
ISBN: 978-1-912713-22-6

To my wonderful children, Emily and Jacob Simpson, the greatest teachers I've ever had. I love you both with all my heart.

To my beautiful, loving, supportive wife Anna Simpson, for your grace and compassion when faced with my many shortcomings. I love you.

To Victoria Simpson, for the gift of you and our children. You are, and will always be, deeply loved.

And in eternal gratitude to my parents, Janet and Peter Simpson, for their countless sacrifices in my name. You are loved and so missed.

Contents

A message to the reader
from the author

*"In times of change learners inherit the earth; while
the learned find themselves beautifully equipped
to deal with a world that no longer exists."*

Eric Hoffer

Dear reader,

This book invites you to a new understanding of what
it means to be a learner—the kind of learner Hoffer
referred to.

We live in times of perpetual and rapid change. Never
have Hoffer's words been so profound.

And never has it been more vital to the understanding
revealed in these pages.

Enjoy the process of becoming more.

~ Christian Simpson, May 2019.

A Conforming Non-Conformist

Mr Cooper wasn't a man to mince his words. He sat across the table from my mother, and just said it like it was: "Mrs Simpson, your boy will sell ice to Eskimos, but unless he starts applying himself to his school work, he'll not amount to much in the classroom."

It was the late 1970s, Mr Cooper was my form teacher at St. Peter's Junior School in Harborne, Birmingham, England, and he'd just delivered the news my mother didn't want to hear. She was born just before the Second World War and her generation, more so than perhaps any other, aspired for a much better way of life than her parents' generation. To my mother, that translated into hopes for a career in white-collar management for her only child—and as far as she was concerned, he needed good academic results to make it happen.

Despite Mr Cooper's recognition of my selling ability, I'm not one of those business owners who started flexing his entrepreneurial muscles early. I wasn't the kid who bought "stuff", added a healthy margin, and sold it to kids in the playground. I didn't set up a car washing business in my neighbourhood, either. I didn't even have a paper round. All I wanted to do was play football, ride my bike, listen to music, and watch girls.

I was thirty-six years old before I became a "real" business owner. I didn't even think of running my own business until I was a couple of years beyond my thirtieth birthday and yet, as I looked back on it years later, my career had demanded a substantial degree of entrepreneurial prowess—even though I was working on someone else's agenda.

We're all products of our environment. In our formative years, we're all heavily influenced by those around us—the products of somebody else's habitual way of thinking. I was no different. Like everyone else, in a few ways the programming of my formative years served me—and in many ways, it didn't. More than a decade after the conversation between Mr Cooper and my mother, I delivered on their respective hopes and prophecy. For seventeen of my nineteen years as an employee, I was in corporate sales roles.

My first job was a cash-in-hand, commission-only role, selling domestic security systems door-to-door on some of England's most unsavoury housing estates. By the end of my employed years, I was earning a healthy six figures selling multi-million-dollar telecommunications solutions to end users via third-party vendors. In between, I'd sold capital equipment and advertising to businesses of all sizes, and financial services—products such as life assurance, pensions, and mortgages to consumers. I never considered myself to be an entrepreneur, and yet to be successful in these roles I had to be one. I was responsible for my own business within someone else's business. My results either stacked up or they didn't—and if they didn't, I would soon be out of a job and income. Looking back, in many ways, I was an entrepreneur waiting to be set free... I just didn't know it back then.

At the time of putting these words down on paper, I've been in the real entrepreneurial game for almost thirteen years, and it's been one hell of a ride. If you're expecting to hear a story of consistent, outstanding success, you'll be disappointed. Being an entrepreneur has been the steepest learning curve of my life. Mine is not the stereotypical "rags to riches" story—yet in those thirteen years, I've tasted the ugliest, darkest, most challenging side of entrepreneurial life, the far more palatable opposite end of the equation, and everything in between.

> **"Life, at every level, is a game of psychology, and there's a science to success in *everything*."**

I've been a spectacular entrepreneurial failure, driving my business into liquidation. I've wallowed in the illusion of comfort accompanying self-deluded mediocrity. And I've built an astonishingly profitable, successful global enterprise.

I've been clueless, naive, and utterly out of my depth at times... and I've also been smart enough to learn from my mistakes and willing to learn from the mistakes of others. I'm sharing my story with you because it's crucial for you to understand the proven methods you're about to discover in this book, and those revealed beyond it, are drawn from a rich tapestry of experience. Life, at every level, is a game of psychology, and there's a science to success in *everything*. Nowhere is this universal truth more apparent than in the "muck 'n' bullets" reality of entrepreneurial life. If you were to ask me to articulate the biggest lesson I've learned in my professional career to date, it would be the stark realisation highly successful entrepreneurs think in an entirely different way to the masses of well-intentioned, hard-working, yet underachieving business owners.

This book is about bridging the gap because believe me, contrary to what most people believe, the gap can be bridged—and I'll prove it. Not just from my own experience (although I hasten to add I'm still a work-in-progress)... and not only from the experience of the highly successful entrepreneurs I've had the privilege of being mentored by, who also addressed the gap at some point in their history... but also by proven, irrefutable, scientific evidence.

This book is about debunking the myths, unravelling the lies, and overcoming the ignorance denying you the wealth, prosperity, and freedom you can have if you're willing to unlearn and relieve yourself of the habitual ways of thinking we've all inherited from our environment. After all, what's the point of spending your entire career taking the risks associated with entrepreneurial life if you're not to enjoy the rewards?

Sadly, this is the reality most business owners face. You won't have to face it, though, if you're willing to discover and act upon the eye-opening truths revealed in these pages—and I don't make claims of this magnitude lightly. You have much to look forward to.

Enjoy the process of becoming more.

Christian Simpson
April 2019

Why This Book Is So Important

"If you work hard on your job, you can make a living. If you work hard on yourself, you can make a fortune."

~ Jim Rohn

You're here because you want more. More from your business, from your life, and from yourself.

Every business owner I know is anxious to improve their circumstances. Some are living lives of quiet desperation; others have reached a comfortable level—then plateaued. A few seem to soar. The vast majority, though, remain stuck in the results they work so desperately hard to change.

Many of these are hard-working, well-intentioned entrepreneurs—yet because they've always done things in a certain way their minds are closed to a different approach.

At best they earn a comfortable living... at worst, their business fails.

So let me ask you: what are your results revealing

to you about you? Where are you creating the kind of success in your business to generate the financial freedom and quality of life you aspire to? Do you secretly suspect the Top 0.1% of business owners possess some quality you're somehow missing?

The Secret Truth You'll Never Hear

Well, here's the biggest truth you'll never hear about entrepreneurial success: the most significant risk to your success is not the state of the economy, the banks, the marketplace, the government, or your competition. **The biggest threat to your entrepreneurial success is thinking as most business owners think.**

We *all* have the potential to achieve outstanding entrepreneurial success. The Top 0.1% are not superhuman, and they're not somehow "different" to mere mortals. They are, for the most part, just like you and me. The problem is, most entrepreneurs do business in precisely the same way as most entrepreneurs do business. And so they struggle... or achieve comfortable mediocrity at best.

Why? Because they model what creates struggle and mediocrity instead of modelling what creates extraordinary entrepreneurial success!

And yet it's not their fault. It's human nature: we're programmed by evolution to look around us at what others are doing, then behave in the same way. This behaviour has kept us alive for aeons.

In many situations, in our social lives and communities, what the majority is doing is the right thing to do. After all, if you can smell smoke, and everyone's heading for the fire exit, you should probably do the same.

Yet in large swathes of life, business included, following the crowd is nothing short of disastrous.

The statistics speak for themselves:

- Nearly half of all businesses fail in the first five years.
- Only 0.1% of business owners are bringing in almost £1 million a year in pre-tax earnings.

In today's fast-changing business environment, if you're going to accomplish more than single-digit profit growth, you must be willing to do whatever it takes to join the minority.

> **"The biggest threat to your success is thinking as most business owners think."**

If you're not willing to do what it takes, I have absolutely no idea how you'll accomplish the kind of success which leads to the financial prosperity, wealth, and freedom that makes taking the entrepreneurial path so worthwhile.

You must be willing to do things most business owners simply won't do. Not can't... *won't*.

You Have Another Choice

You don't have to follow the well-trodden path to struggle and mediocrity. There is another choice for you—and this book is where it all changes. What's revealed in these pages are the powerful and proven principles representing the central tenets of the ultimate entrepreneurial success strategy.

Here are three things you need to know straight away:

1. The most successful entrepreneurs were not born with any more talent, potential, wealth,

resources, or "luck" than you and me.

2. Their success has come from deliberately thinking differently to how most business owners think.

3. You can make the same choice.

If you doubt any of this, you only have to look around you. During economic downturns there are businesses which not only survive, they thrive—yet they're exposed to the same derogatory market conditions as every other company.

The difference in these businesses is not luck, fortune, or favour; it's the quality of thinking the business owner brings to the business. 99.9% of business owners stay on the familiar, comfortable treadmill, stuck in habitual ways of thinking, engaging in the same systematic activities, recreating similar results over and over while hoping for something to change.

You don't have to follow their lead. You don't have to follow the herd to their statistically proven miserable outcomes.

You can choose a different path, a far more profitable, prosperous, and profitable one—you just need to be willing to think differently.

Why There Are So Few Entrepreneurial Millionaires

There's an excellent reason why, up until now, just 0.1% of business owners earn £1 million a year. And there's an excellent reason why this statistic hasn't changed since it was first measured in the mid-1950s. If you spend even a short amount of time in the company of highly successful entrepreneurs, you'll soon appreciate they have a very different worldview than the vast majority of business owners.

Here are three simple examples of how the Top 0.1% think differently:

1. The Top 0.1% understand their business growth can only reflect the quality of their thinking—so they deliberately invest time and money in improving and challenging the way they think.

2. They focus on improvement, not activity. The Top 0.1% work at the cause, not the effect, of their performance.

3. The Top 0.1% develop the owner not the business. They understand their personal growth determines their success. The quote at the top of this section, by Jim Rohn,

> **"The Top 0.1% develop the owner not the business."**

sums it up nicely. To achieve success in any area of life, you need to develop yourself first.

Now, if you believe you already think differently from 99.9% of hard-working entrepreneurs, yet you're getting the same kind of results they are despite all the blood, sweat, and tears you put into your business, you may want to think again.

Chances are, your reality may be painting a different picture—a picture borne out by the fact you've come to these words now, and you know things are not going to plan.

The question you need answering is whether you're willing to do anything about it. Because I guarantee if you embrace any of the ideas I'm sharing with you in this book and put them into action via the proven, transformational coaching resources you now have at your disposal, your results—not just in your business, in every area of life you want to see transformation—will improve dramatically.

Again, I don't make claims of this magnitude lightly. This is about personal and professional transformation. Everything you're about to discover in these pages has been tested and proven by my clients and me over the years in bust and boom economic cycles. In fact, these principles are the only way to immunise your business and personal life from the influence of external market forces such as economic swings, competition, and meddling politicians.

I'm sure you've heard all this before. After all, the world isn't short of people who promise much yet deliver little, if anything. And on every corner, some snake-oil salesman lurks, vowing to share the great secrets of life and success with you.

So I'm not expecting you to take my word for it naively. I'm not asking you to blindly accept all I put before you. Yes, I promise much. And I deliver much more than I pledge. If I didn't, I wouldn't be entering my third decade in this industry with the reputation and credibility I have.

As I lead you to a whole new level of understanding and the results arising from it, understand this: I'm not asking you to trust me—we don't know each other yet. I'm asking you to *test* me. Which brings me to another vital matter...

Whom You Learn From Matters

This book is about you, not me. That said, I learned a long time ago whom you learn from is more important than what you learn. You might not know me from

Adam, so as you're about to invest time (the only thing you inexorably spend and cannot earn) in reading this powerful material, it pays to know you're investing your time wisely. And you start by ensuring you're in the right hands.

So what I'm about to share with you by way of an introduction isn't from a position of conceit or self-promotion. What you think of me is not my business or concern. My concern is what you think of my ability to help you.

If you're to enjoy the kind of success eluding most business owners, you'll need to open up to ideas and ways of thinking which may seem counter-intuitive—even contrarian—to what you've been programmed to believe about yourself, other people, life, and what it takes to enjoy greater success. You'll never be able to open up to another way of thinking unless you believe you're receiving these new ideas from a credible source.

I can't claim to be gifted at many things. However, what I am gifted in, I'm world class at. My areas of expertise have allowed me to become a leading global authority in my industry.

First and foremost, I'm the world's highest-paid professionally qualified coach, and the world's leading coach and mentor in the psychology of success and wealth generation to business owners and entrepreneurs.

Not only am I one of the most sought-after professional coaches on the planet; I'm also recognised as a subject matter expert in the field of coaching.

I created both The Simpson Method of Transformational Coaching™ and The Maxwell Method of Coaching, and to date, I've personally trained more than 30,000 people to the highest standards in the professional coaching industry.

Moreover, my credibility in the eyes of my industry peers, including many of the "big hitters", is not just because my body of work is so effective and the results my clients get are off the charts—it's also because I've lived the methods I teach.

I transformed my own life using the methods I now share with others, long before I brought them to the attention of business owners like you. This sums up precisely what you can expect from me: a grounded, down-to-earth, say-it-like-it-is, matter-of-fact integrity, authenticity, and congruence.

So, while many of the ideas I share with you will unquestionably seem foreign to your current way of thinking, if you're on the hunt for mind-boggling, nonsensical psycho-babble and unsubstantiated pseudoscience, I'm not the man for you, and you'll be bitterly disappointed.

There's an excellent reason why so many business owners, multi-millionaire "big guns", and the major players in my industry pay me so handsomely for my services (after all, they're very well-connected people who aren't struggling to find talented subject-matter experts who'd bend over backwards to work with them).

> "Our idols aren't truly idols at all. They're simply ordinary people doing extraordinary things."

They choose me because my methods get profound results for people. And in entrepreneurial life, results are all that matter.

In the last decade alone, the strategies you're about to discover have transformed the lives of business owners in more than 160 countries, so be assured of this: if you're willing to help yourself and put your back into these proven methods and resources, you'll be rewarded exponentially for the rest of your days. That, I can personally guarantee.

Which brings me to another crucial point. One of our greatest shortcomings is we're programmed to look up to successful people, rather than look into them. We idolise them, place them on a pedestal, elevate and glorify them. Is it any wonder we so often find ourselves convinced their achievements are so beyond our own capabilities?

In our misplaced exaltation, is it any wonder we lose or limit our ability to learn from them? Is it a surprise we fail to model and emulate what they're doing? In elevating the most successful people in such a way, their achievements seem so far away from the present conditions and circumstances of our lives, we can't imagine doing the same as them.

To use a prominent example we can all relate to, consider Jesus Christ. Whatever your beliefs, you know billions glorify him—or at least the idea of him—yet fail to hear and live into the message the man brought to the world.

Jesus is positioned as the "one and only Son of God", elevated to untouchable and unquestionable heights, rather than being seen as the highly conscious individual he was. Christ became unreachable, and as a consequence, everything he stood for, taught and demonstrated to enlighten and empower humanity from the tyranny of its own ignorance was not only lost, it's been contorted ever since. Our idols aren't truly idols at all. They're simply ordinary people doing extraordinary things. In other words, they think and act differently to the masses.

It's natural we look up to those we admire—and we must look into them, too. We can emulate their success by modelling what they do to build the life we intend for ourselves.

Take Back Control for Yourself

You won't be subjected to a host of impractical abstract theories. Thousands of entrepreneurs can testify to the transformational impact of the proven methods contained in these pages.

Some who came my way were already highly successful. You might wonder why that would be. You won't be wondering by the end of this book. For now, let's just say these people have developed an understanding of themselves as the cause of all their effects, and most importantly of all, they live into that truth. They're conscious entrepreneurs who understand what few business owners understand: life doesn't give you what you want, it gives you who you are.

> "This book exists because 99.9% of business owners start in the wrong place... and it shows, in their results."

Others came to me utterly frustrated. They'd built their business to the point of not having to worry about when and how the next bill was going to be paid... yet regardless of the level of success they found themselves at, they couldn't get beyond a certain point in their growth. They knew there was more, they knew there was a way out, but they couldn't see the wood for the trees. They were stuck. And it doesn't matter if you're stuck at $100,000 a year or $100,000 a minute: if you're stuck, you're stuck—and stuck stinks.

Many came to me in desperate circumstances, struggling with a business which sapped all their time, money, and energy for little, if any, return—just to keep their heads above water or maintain a lifestyle they'd get if they worked for someone else.

One by one, regardless of where they stood on the ladder between significance, success, struggle and failure, they adopted the methods you're about to discover and not only turned things around, they dramatically transformed their lives for the better.

They now own self-managing, self-multiplying ventures generating ever-increasing profits for ever-increasing personal prosperity.

Most importantly of all, they've won back their personal lives and are free to focus on what brings meaning to them: their health and wellbeing, relationships, more time and money to enjoy the people and things they value most.

And here's the point: they haven't done this by focusing on the business. Not by building new systems. Or buying new software. Or jumping on the latest marketing fads and "ninja tactics" from the latest self-anointed, self-appointed "Guru".

No—they owe their success to one thing and one thing only: their willingness to unlearn habitual ways of thinking to dramatically improve the quality of thinking they're bringing to every area of life.

Like all the business owners who come to my body of work and put it into practice, they discover how to increasingly unlock more of the untapped potential within the most powerful asset they'll ever own: their minds.

Consequently, as results improve dramatically, their priorities change. Their focus shifts 180 degrees.

> **"Your business will never outgrow the quality of thinking you bring to it."**

They choose to develop the owner, not the business.

And make no mistake: if you're to be all you're capable of becoming, not just as an entrepreneur but also as a human being—so you can enjoy the wealth, freedom and prosperity of the so-called entrepreneurial dream—you have to make the same choice.

Start In the Right Place

This book exists because 99.9% of business owners start in the wrong place... and it shows, in their results.

They focus on improving the business, never themselves. Your success depends on you switching those priorities around.

I guarantee if you develop the owner, not the business, your business will perpetually grow and thrive as a consequence. Your business will never outgrow you. It'll never outgrow the quality of thinking you bring to it. If improving the quality of the thinking you bring to your business isn't a priority in your life, don't expect your business to grow in spite of you. Life just doesn't roll that way.

You have in your hand a book containing information and resources which will serve you for the rest of your days, regardless of the level of success you're at.

It's not a book you read once then dispense of. You don't complete or graduate from this material, and I strongly encourage you to read it often—at least a couple of times a year.

Every time you do, you'll get new, powerful and profitable insights. Of course, the content of the book won't have changed at all, *you* will have changed—you'll come back

"There's an 'L' before earning..."

to this information at a higher level of awareness after putting these ideas to work.

You'll pick up on concepts you didn't see before because at your previous level of consciousness you weren't ready to receive them.

Given you have this book in your hand, and you're paying attention to its contents, I don't need to question your interest in greater success in life.

Instead, I encourage you to approach this book somewhat differently to how you probably read other books. Make sure you're free from potential distractions. Make it known you don't want to be interrupted for the time you're dedicating to it and, most importantly, answer the coaching questions in each chapter and in the Success Implementation Guide™ honestly.

Keep notes on your progress. I'm not in the business of making busy people busier, and I've no intention of adding activities to what I'm sure is already a full life. However, not all actions are equal, and I can assure you this book, and the information and questions within it, are the key to open the door to the success you aspire to.

Intellectually grasping these concepts is not difficult. Yes, the information is powerful, but unless it's put to use through the associated coaching questions, reading it will be a futile exercise. It's not about what you know, it's about what you do.

Old habits die hard. We are always at risk of slipping back into old habits and old ways of thinking. There's an "L" before earning, and learning isn't an event—it's an ongoing process. The more successful you become, the bigger the challenges you'll face. And the bigger the challenges you face, the "bigger" you need to be on the inside to overcome them.

This is life's way of teaching you the universal truth I mentioned before: life doesn't give what you want, it gives you who you are.

Every challenge, every drawback, every mistake and perceived failure is life bringing you the opportunity to grow into the person you need to become to create your desired outcome. So as you grow through this process (which you will) remember you might become frustrated at times because you'll meet new challenges and new areas for development. Embrace them with open arms, because I promise you, they'll make you into the person you intend to become.

Many myths surround extraordinary entrepreneurial success and what creates it, and I'm about to put many of them to bed by sharing irrefutable scientific evidence and well-documented research dispelling most, if not all, those myths.

My promise to you is this: if—and *only* if—you're willing to master and consistently apply a surprisingly small number of easily grasped strategies to your business, then regardless of the so-called competition, state of the economy, or tinkering of self-serving politicians, the truth is you can enjoy extraordinary business success and everything accompanying it… you just need to be shown how.

It's a bold promise, for sure—and it's one I make without reservation. So if you're new to my work, and you're somewhat sceptical or reserved, remember: I'm not asking you to trust me. I'm asking you to test me.

Putting Carts Before Horses: What Does Success Mean To You?

"We like to think of our champions and idols as superheroes who were born different from us. We don't like to think of them as relatively ordinary people who made themselves extraordinary."

Carol Dweck

I think really successful entrepreneurs like Chris, you know, the ones who become millionaires, they're born with abilities the rest of us just don't have."

We'd only just met. It was early 2013, and this was the first few minutes of a two-day entrepreneurial event held by a very successful business owner, exclusively for his high-end clients.

I smiled at the lady I was talking with.

"What brings you here, to this event?" I asked.

She initially looked a little taken aback at my question, as if her reasons were blatantly obvious—and replied she was there to learn how to become more successful. My curiosity got the better of me again, and another question followed.

"I understand. So what's true for you then? That you can learn to be far more successful, or highly successful people are born with abilities the rest of us just don't have?"

The contradiction may be evident to you and me, but it wasn't apparent to the lady concerned. We've all experienced being oblivious to the obvious. After all, it's hard to see the picture when you're in the frame.

This lady's opinion isn't uncommon, and unless she changes her thinking by modifying her beliefs, very little will change for her. Yes, she'll put herself in seminars, workshops, and events like the one where I met her. And she'll be exposed to a lot of potent information to help grow her business—but I guarantee she won't put much, if any of it, to work. Her current belief system will undermine and sabotage everything she does—and the worst part is, she won't even be aware of it.

Our beliefs are the architects of our results. Beliefs sponsor habitual ways of thinking and drive our behaviour. Sadly, for the vast majority (if not all) our waking hours, we're on autopilot, thinking the same thoughts, doing the same things... and we're not aware it's happening.

> **"Our beliefs are the architects of our results."**

In other words, for most, if not all of our days, we're not consciously participating in the creation of our results. I don't think it's possible to exaggerate how much of a threat this belief system is to your success.

The fundamental message this book brings to you is this: everything starts with you and the quality of your thinking. Nothing will change for the better until the quality of your thinking improves.

And if your quality of thinking is to improve, you need to understand how you think and, most importantly, what sponsors the current level of thinking you're bringing to your life.

Before we go any further, let's examine some irrefutable evidence to confirm why this is so vital to your success.

Generations of Statistics Don't Lie

The statistics revealing the realities of entrepreneurial life can differ from source to source. However, regardless of where you look, they all make for particularly unpleasant reading. The bottom line is, if you run your own business, you're far more likely to fail than succeed. And, even if you don't fail, you're far more likely to struggle than thrive. That's the bad news.

"Your psychological blueprint cannot be outperformed. It can, however, be modified."

But there's excellent news, too. The overwhelming majority of business owners struggle and underachieve not because they lack talent, potential, resources, or ability. It's because they've been programmed for struggle and underachievement by their environment. We are all products of our environment. We all carry a psychological "blueprint" determining our level of success in every aspect of our lives. This "blueprint" cannot be outperformed. It can, however, be modified.

I've proved this in my own life, and I've confirmed it, through the work I do, in the lives of thousands of other business owners. Which means—and this is the excellent news—your success is entirely in your hands.

You have the power to succeed regardless of external market forces, conditions, or circumstances. It's merely a matter of reprogramming or, to be more precise, unlearning.

It all starts by taking control of the greatest asset you'll ever have at your disposal—the asset creating your reality, whether you're conscious in the act of creation or not. That asset is your mind.

The Truth About Wealth Most Business Owners Will Never Know

Name a profession where there's not at least some level of education to equip a person for success in their role. A career where a person just dives in and hopes for the best. Here's one—the humble entrepreneur.

The only education we entrepreneurs get is the day-to-day reality of running the business. When your entire life, from your income and bank balance, to the health, wealth, and wellbeing of your family, is dependant on you and the success of your business, it's one hell of a risk to take. Risk is all very well if it brings a much higher return, but as we've already seen, this is not how life stacks up for the vast majority of business owners. For the majority, it's all risk and no reward.

What's the point in taking on all the extra responsibility this career choice demands if the wealth and freedom of the entrepreneurial dream remain on a distant horizon? Why take on all the additional responsibility and burden of running the business you're effectively an employee in?

We all start with daring hopes and expansive dreams. None of us set out with the intention to struggle. Who in their right mind would consciously choose to be average, spending a life wallowing in abject mediocrity and underachievement? And who deliberately creates the monster which consumes a life, working harder and harder for longer and longer just to maintain a certain standard of living? I've yet to meet a business owner with those specific objectives, yet I've met countless thousands who live that reality every day. So what happens in the gap between those first heady days of starting a business and where most business owners end up?

It's Not the Business...

Every entrepreneur is a business owner, but not every business owner is an entrepreneur. It's no exaggeration to say most business owners own a job, not a business.

The problem is never the business. The problem is the way the owner thinks. A business can never outgrow the quality of thinking the owner brings to it. There's a science to everything and success is no different.

> **"A business can never outgrow the quality of thinking the owner brings to it."**

Sadly, only a small percentile of the population—statistically the Top 0.1%—are willing to do what's necessary, to the degree it's required. Only the Top 0.1% are willing to unlearn the habitual ways of thinking keeping the vast majority chained to the struggle, mediocrity, and underachievement they claim to want to end. Only the Top 0.1% were willing to modify their psychological blueprint to create the wealth, prosperity, and freedom making it all worthwhile.

Of course, there's far more to a wealthy life than

money alone. However, money, if used intelligently, is the great enabler of entrepreneurial wealth and freedom—so it's reasonable to use money as an easily identifiable benchmark for success.

And The Numbers Aren't What You Think

Much attention is given to the area of the socio-economic pyramid called the Top 1%, yet on both sides of the Atlantic, the income required to qualify for this group is surprisingly low. In the UK, according to official data by the Office of National Statistics and HMRC (both in 2015-16), the pre-tax earnings figure for the Top 1% is just £170,000 per year.

In the US (according to data from a 2014 report by professors Fatih Guvenen, Greg Kaplan and Jae Song, adjusted for 2018 inflation rates by personal finance writer Sam Dogen of Financial Samurai) the figure ranges from $160,000 at age 25, $320,000 at age 40, to just $470,000 by the age of 50. If this doesn't surprise and inspire you in equal measure, it should. The benchmark to be in the Top 1% is astonishingly low.

Wealth is a choice—one too few make. Wealth goes far beyond financial success alone, yet you can't deny the modest income levels it takes to qualify for the Top 1% will not bring the life-changing rewards promised by the entrepreneurial dream.

Forget the Top 1%. Set your intentions much higher. I can assure you, it's more than possible for you if you're willing to grasp and, most importantly, live into the principles set out in this book. Yes, it's going to be counter-intuitive. Yes, it'll be uncomfortable and challenging at times. And yes, you might struggle to appreciate the link between your actions and your results—until everything starts to change for the better.

The bottom line is this: the Top 0.1% earn on average £990,000 per year before tax, and if you're to do the same—or a hell of a lot more—you need to think and act as the Top 0.1% do. So where do you start?

Modifying Your Psychological Blueprint

You start with yourself, not the business. The ultimate entrepreneurial success strategy—and the all-important foundational first pillar in *The 4 Pillars of Mastery*™—is **develop the owner not the business**.

For the vast majority of business owners, it represents a complete 180-degree shift in how they go about their day-to-day lives. Your business is a vehicle through which you extract profit to shape life on your own terms. If your business is to generate the profits you need to make yourself wealthy, without devouring the life you lead today and denying the quality of life you aspire to lead in the future, you must do more than intellectually grasp this principle.

I've said it before—and I'm happy to repeat it—your business cannot outgrow the quality of thinking you bring to it.

You've spent a lifetime being moulded into one of the 99.9%. This book will enable you to grow into one of the Top 0.1%. You're about to elevate the quality of thinking you bring to your business so you can think, act, and achieve like the Top 0.1%.

- In Chapter 1, we'll start with education. You'll discover why most of us are so ill-equipped to create successful businesses—and how to begin

31

undoing all the damage.

- Chapter 2 will turn your ideas of intelligence upside down, and show you why you can succeed in your business regardless of your IQ.
- Chapter 3 reveals the truth and dispels the myths about your potential: what it is, what it isn't, and how to tap into limitless resources lying undiscovered within you.
- Chapter 4 takes you on a journey through success: you'll discover what the most successful people in the business world attribute to their success, and how you can start creating your success blueprint.
- And finally, you'll discover what you can do next to continue your journey of mastery.

Take note, though: you're not on a passive journey of discovery. Although the proven principles in this book will bring eye-opening perspectives and open up a door to a plethora of possibilities in your marvellous yet grossly underused mind, only you can walk through that door.

You won't just be hearing about the Top 0.1% of entrepreneurs who have already made it. You'll also be hearing from business owners on the same journey you are—business owners who have been working with me as coaching clients and as students of the ultimate entrepreneurial success strategy and the rest of *The 4 Pillars of Mastery*™. There is nothing more powerful, or credible, to prove the explicit promise I've made to you about the transformational impact of these proven ideas, than the testimonies of those who've already put them to work and reaped the rewards accordingly.

I asked a handful of my clients to share their stories

with you so you can be assured the time you invest in these pages is spent wisely. Throughout this book, you'll be prompted to download your Success Implementation Guide™. Within it are the all-important coaching questions I referred to earlier, with plenty of space to record your answers. The questions are not a test; they're the difference makers, highly effective in improving the quality of thinking you bring to your business and personal life.

Do not be tempted to skip the questions. They're by far the most crucial part of all the resources at your disposal. To use a simple analogy: at a glance, a building can appear to draw its strength from the bricks in its walls, when in fact it's the mortar holding the bricks in place making the structure robust.

> "The most costly ignorance of all is ignorance of self."

The same principle applies to this body of work and the questions I'm asking you. These fundamental lines of enquiry are carefully and deliberately structured to internalise the strategies within this book, ensuring you put them to work in your business and personal life.

The questions raise your self-awareness, elevate your consciousness, and fill the gap between what you know and what you do. And that's what gets results.

Creating Your Success

Here's what I can guarantee about you: you're ignorant. I am, you are, we all are. Humanity is ignorant.

To varying degrees, every single one of us is ignorant—we just don't know some things. Ignorance is unconsciousness, the opposite of awareness. The most costly ignorance of all is ignorance of self.

One of the most challenging things for human beings to do is stand in front of the proverbial mirror and take an honest assessment of themselves. Equally as challenging for most of humanity is the acceptance of themselves as the creator of their outcomes, for with such an understanding comes total responsibility and ownership of your life. For many, it's too difficult a pill to swallow. It requires courage to "know thyself". It takes guts to go within, to self-improve, to master oneself. Yet the price of not doing so is the highest price of all.

Your business and personal success will always be in direct proportion to how much you're willing to go within. Most people are oblivious to this truth, or they're unwilling to go there, which is why their greatest aspirations never transpire into tangible results. They talk a good game but walk a lame one. As Oli Fisher, an English entrepreneur whose Florida-based flying school, Pilots Paradise, has grown significantly as a consequence of putting these ideas to work, recently told me: "The Four Pillars is an interesting process because not everyone is ready to look at themselves this deeply. For the right people, it will help them grow."

At this juncture, the only question calling for an answer is: how willing are you to grow? How willing are you to go to the uncharted territory within, where your untapped potential awaits conscious recognition, so you can become all you're capable of becoming?

How willing are you to unlearn a lifetime of programming for struggle, mediocrity and underachievement? How willing are you to not just read and discover, but to reflect, evaluate and think into much greater results?

I might not know you personally, but I don't need to. Many years and thousands of hours helping human beings work on their "inner game" has given me the experience to say this with unshakeable authority: you are capable of so much more than even your highest aspirations.

This isn't some shallow motivational claim; it's a cast-iron truth. You can be all you aspire to be—and more.

The only question to ask is: *will you*?

Chapter 1

Undoing Indoctrination

"Education consists mainly of what we have unlearned."

~ Mark Twain

A few years ago, I was with a business associate of mine. We were driving to his home in Jupiter Island, Florida. This man is a great thinker, one of the most successful entrepreneurs I know, and we were discussing his latest business venture.

His most recent project generated just over US$10 million in its first year. No small beer.

When I asked him what the most significant lesson from his entrepreneurial career to date was, he replied instantly: "I've learned that if my business is only as good as my current thinking, it's in trouble." Intrigued, I asked him to elaborate.

He said, "Christian, the world stops for no-one. If I'm not working to improve how I think into my results, this business is going backwards. I have a great team around me, and I've made sure they understand this principle: if they're not growing, we're not growing. And if I'm not growing, they're not growing. So it may sound counterintuitive to some, but my main focus isn't the business. It's my thinking."

It will sound counterintuitive, not just to some; to many. The bottom line is: highly successful people understand that just as a ship can only gain direction from its captain and crew, a business can only reflect its owner's quality of thinking.

Perhaps you're shaking your head and thinking, "Well, this is blatantly obvious! I already knew that." And I'm sure you did. But let me ask you something: how much time, effort, and money have you invested in improving how you think recently? How much time, effort, and money have you invested in personal growth—so you can be, do, and have more in your life?

I'm not talking about new skills or academic business qualifications. The world is full of empty suits with MBAs. I'm talking about self-education. I'm talking about improving yourself at the level of your character. Contrary to popular opinion, your character isn't fixed, unable to be improved. "It's just the way he is, he'll never change!" is only true if the individual concerned allows it to be true.

I wasn't taught to think, self-reflect, and self-evaluate at home or school. Consequently, like most kids, I grew up believing some people were more intelligent than others, and you made the best of what you had from the "genetic lottery". It's likely to be the same for you. It shouldn't surprise you, then, that until this point you've not prioritised improving your self-awareness and raising your consciousness, so the quality of thinking you bring to your life is at a different level than it was before. If you've never prioritised self-education, never considered it, or done very little of it, you're not alone. The vast majority of business owners haven't either—and it shows, in their results. I'm no different. I didn't prioritise self-education, either—it didn't cross my mind. I was programmed to think success came from achieving good grades in school and college, acquiring some job-related skills and qualifications, and earning letters after my name. Maybe you were programmed in a similar way. Most of us are. Nobody told me I could improve my thinking. Nobody explained the need for personal growth. Nobody pointed out character attributes will ultimately determine my level of success, not good grades or qualifications.

It's why I spent far too many years following the well-trodden path. It's why I spent far too long working a j-o-b, operating on someone else's agenda, making someone else rich. And it's why I spent far too much time doing work that filled my bank account while emptying my soul.

Educated Into Mediocrity

If you're a product of the same kind of education system as I am, you'll have spent your formative years being taught *what* to think, not *how* to think. We're taught to cram facts and figures into our minds. We're shown how to pass exams and solve mathematical problems. And we're told to analyse what authors might have meant when writing the world's great works of fiction.

Unless we were fortunate, our teachers—who waded through the same education system as you and me—taught us the curriculum and did their best... however, like other authority figures in our lives, they failed to equip us to go within, to self-discover, to think inductively into our truth rather than just blindly accept established norms and ideas. They knew no better, because no authority figure in their lives taught them to go within during their formative years—and you cannot give what you don't have. There wasn't a class on entrepreneurial skills or how to live successfully on my curriculum, and I bet there wasn't on yours. I don't know of a single successful entrepreneur who attributes their success in life and in business to what they learned at school. In fact, most of the highly successful business owners I know either dropped out of the education system early or were classroom dummies. Academia wasn't their forte.

And they didn't learn their craft in business schools or adult education establishments either, because those institutions follow the same limited learning model. Completing an MBA is commendable, but it doesn't guarantee you'll be a success in business. The number of unemployed or underachieving MBA graduates is a testament to that.

No, as insane as it unquestionably is, the only education we entrepreneurs get regarding being an entrepreneur is—well, being an entrepreneur. We all learn on the job and, for the most part, we learn by trial and error. Given our entire livelihood is at stake, it's a costly, and often fatal, approach to business.

Entrepreneurship is a perilous business, and the statistics prove it. Just over 50% of companies survive to the end of their first five years, and a large proportion of those who do survive are struggling.

Even more revealing, if not alarming, is the fact that just 0.1% of business owners are millionaires, a statistic which hasn't changed since it was first measured in the mid-1950s. If that doesn't prove we're not getting it right, I don't know what does.

Where's Your Current Mindset Taking You?

We're not just up against the programming of our formal education. We're also up against the mindset instilled in us from birth. As I've already mentioned, we are all products of our environment—products of someone else's habitual way of thinking.

As Oliver Wendell Holmes, Jr. observed, "We are all tattooed in our cradles with the beliefs of our tribe; the record may seem superficial, but it is indelible. You cannot educate a man wholly out of superstitious fears which were implanted in his imagination, no matter how utterly his reason may reject them."

If you've ever wondered why the man-made, fear-based theological constructions of mankind's religions have persisted through the ages, despite the insanity and carnage they've sponsored, you now have your answer.

Most of us are fortunate enough to have parents who loved us dearly and intentionally gave us their best. That said, without question, our parents also unintentionally gave us their worst, projecting ideas into us they inherited from their own upbringing. Ideas which limited them and us, and do not serve us in living a far more successful life.

> **"We are all tattooed in our cradles with the beliefs of our tribe."**
> **~ Oliver Wendell Holmes**

It's not our parents' fault. They literally knew no

better, just as we won't know better as parents unless we're willing to go within and evaluate some of the ideas we hold to be true. What we don't evaluate, challenge, and modify in ourselves, our kids inherit.

And our results, in every aspect of our lives, will be affected by those shortcomings. If we want to improve our results, we need to modify what's producing them—and the buck stops with our beliefs.

Carol Dweck, Professor of Psychology at Stanford University, tested a diverse sample of people while writing her book, *Mindset*, and discovered around 40% of people seemed more inclined toward a growth mindset and 40% seemed more inclined toward a fixed mindset. The other 20% were undecided.

According to Professor Dweck, a growth mindset is the belief intelligence, creative ability, and talent can change. People with a growth mindset believe they can improve their performance through persistence, learning, and critical thinking.

Those with a fixed mindset, however, believe intelligence and talent are fixed at birth, and cannot be significantly changed. These people, then, see failure as demonstrating a lack of ability.

It's the difference between, "You're so talented, I could never do something like that!" and "You did brilliantly—how can I learn to do it too?" And, according to Professor Dweck's research, we have a roughly 40% chance of growing up with a fixed mindset.

In the introduction, I told you the story of the business owner who believed the Top 0.1% of entrepreneurs are somehow special and different from the rest of us. The lady I met, despite putting herself in an environment conducive to growth, was operating with a fixed mindset. I'm sure you can see how the limitations of her mindset sponsored the limitation in her thinking which ultimately limits her success in life.

How about you? What do you *choose* to believe about your ability to join the Top 0.1%? Note the operative word in the question is "choose". Make no mistake: wealth, prosperity, and freedom are a choice; just as poverty, struggle, mediocrity and underachievement are a choice.

Before moving onto the next chapter, stay in the question for a while. Be honest with yourself as you think because, I assure you, your honesty will put you in good stead for what's about to come. Keep your answers in mind as you read on.

Never Underestimate The Power Of External Forces Influencing Your Thoughts

While the success saboteurs lurking undiscovered in the unconscious territories within our minds represent the greatest threat to our growth objectives, they are not alone. There are profoundly damaging external influences plaguing our psychology—the media being the most prominent.

We live in a 24/7 media culture. Every day, our senses are bombarded with an astonishing array of negative news feeds, messages, ideas, and images which are derogatory to success and wellbeing. Until now you might not have given much thought to the consequences of your exposure to the mainstream media.

Most people don't. Most people don't give a second thought to the cause and effect relationship between what they eat and their physical shape and health, so it shouldn't come as a surprise to realise most people never consider the consequences of what they expose their minds to, and the results it generates.

Understand this: how the mind is fed shapes the life that's led. "GIGO" is an acronym used in computer science and mathematics to describe the principle of "garbage in, garbage out". In other words, the quality of output is always determined by the quality of input. This is a natural law. It's a universal principle expressing itself, and the same principle applies to you and your mind. Is it any wonder mental illness is so rife in our society? Is it any wonder helplessness, victim mentality, and entitlement attitudes are on the rise? The vast majority of what the media engine pumps out undermines confidence, cripples dreams, and feeds anxiety, stress, and depression. Ignore this at your peril. You can't afford to underestimate the power of the forces influencing your thoughts—both internal (the unconscious belief systems in your mind) and external (like the media, governments, religions, and any other sources you assign authority to in your life).

Never more than now has the Buddha's warning to "Guard well your thoughts!" been so vital to your success. The media literally programmes the unsuspecting masses to think and act in a certain way—and look where it gets people.

You might think it's difficult to remove yourself from the constant onslaught of negativity. It's not always easy to close your ears to the people around you who claim to be "stuck" and who play the "blame game", pointing fingers at "bad luck" or at someone or something else. I can assure you, switching off from the negativity is easier than you might think.

As you adopt the ultimate entrepreneurial success strategy, put it to work in your life, and continue to do the same with the proven strategies in the rest of *The 4 Pillars of Mastery*™, you'll become increasingly aware of what influences your inner world.

You'll become increasingly adept at evaluating the consequences of the ideas you're exposed to from internal and external sources, including the company you keep. You won't be uninformed. If specific information is important enough, believe me—you'll get to know about it.

Understand this: the Top 0.1% don't ignore what's going on around them. They're mindful as to what they're seeing, reading, or hearing. And they're conscious about how the information they take in affects how they think and act into life.

You can do the same. You *have* to. Otherwise, you'll never become all you're capable of becoming.

Unlearning The Thinking Keeping You Chained

This chapter began with an insightful piece of wisdom from Mark Twain. He had an interesting take on education, believing it consists mainly of what we have "unlearned".

On the face of it, the idea education is a process of "unlearning" seems counterintuitive to us. Surely, education is about learning? And of course, it is—just not in the way you and I have been programmed to think it is. You're about to discover precisely what Twain was referring to. Success in life is more about unlearning the habitual ways of thinking keeping the masses chained to struggle, mediocrity, and underachievement than it ever is about learning new information.

The more you examine the fundamental differences between highly successful entrepreneurs and everyone else—the masses of well-intentioned business owners who work their backsides off only to, at best, create an average business generating just enough profit to make a living—the more you'll see the wisdom in Mark Twain's remarks.

Let's start with the basics. At school, we were programmed to believe we need to be busy. If we were staring off into space, we were reprimanded for daydreaming. By the time we get to working life, we're programmed to get busy doing "stuff".

Standard business practice for ordinary business owners is getting busy getting busy. Activity is king. It feels "right" to be busy in the business and on the business because we're conditioned to associate being busy with being successful.

Normal business practice for highly successful business owners is thinking. Improvement is king. They're driven to get better. They prioritise personal growth and improving their thinking over endless, frantic activity in and on the business. This isn't the only difference between highly successful people and less successful people—but it is the most critical.

And it's why this first pillar in *The 4 Pillars of Mastery*™ is the ultimate entrepreneurial success strategy: develop the owner, not the business.

Develop the Owner, Not the Business

Again, if this sounds counterintuitive, I understand. After all, the business is essential. It's the vehicle through which you derive your financial success and shape life on your own terms. Which is precisely why this 180-degree shift in your thinking is so imperative.

Make no mistake: if you're to enjoy a level of success most business owners will never know, you can't afford to do what most people do and get this the wrong way around.

> **"You can't escape the cause and effect relationship between the quality of your thinking and your results."**

You can't afford to prioritise the business over yourself. Remember: your business and the quality of life it sponsors can never, and will never, outgrow the quality of thinking you bring to it. For the average business owner, getting busy doing "the job" takes priority over self-improvement and personal growth every day of the week. It's why they're average.

You can't escape the cause and effect relationship between the quality of your thinking and your results. Yet only a small percentage of business owners deliberately prioritise daily activities which challenge, stretch, and improve how they think into their results.

What about you? When was the last time you deliberately made it a priority to improve how you think? And when has it ever been a priority in your day?

Because I can assure you, you can dramatically improve the quality of thinking you bring to your personal and professional life. All you need are the tools, resources and expertise to help you do it, which is precisely what you have here.

If this is all new to you, and changing your thinking never even crossed your mind, resist the urge to judge yourself. After all, you'll never seek to improve what you're not aware can be improved. On the contrary, celebrate the fact you're now aware of just how vital this change is, and now you have the life-changing opportunity to do something about it. Most business owners don't have that privilege. Unless they come to this body of work, they'll remain oblivious to this great truth. They'll spend their entire lives never knowing the creative power of their own thoughts and their ability to transform their results as a consequence of transforming how they think.

Some say insanity is doing the same things over and over again while expecting different results. I don't consider such behaviour to be insane. However, repeating the same activities and expecting better outcomes is undoubtedly the dumbest game there is— and the sad truth is, the game is common.

I'm not suggesting activity isn't important—we all know thinking isn't enough on its own, and we all know we have to act into our success—yet this commonly held idea success comes from hard work and hard work alone is flawed. After all, if it all took was hard work, the vast majority of industrious business owners would be living the entrepreneurial dream already... and they're not.

The only reason they're not living the entrepreneurial dream is they mostly work hard at the least effective activities. They're busy spinning the hamster wheel just to stand still and keep their heads above water.

As the sad statistics of entrepreneurial life reveal, when it comes to what it takes to enjoy the kind of success making this choice of career worthwhile, the undeniable truth is most business owners aren't working on the most critical activities. Improving the quality of their thinking is the most essential activity of all.

Improve Your Thinking to Improve Your Results

Understand this: specific activities have a disproportionate impact on results. In other words, certain things we *could* do are far more effective than many things we *actually* do.

It's not an exaggeration to say most people spend far too much time immersed in activities having little or no impact on creating greater success in their lives. And most spend far too little time on activities that do.

We human beings like to operate within the confines of comfort, rather than engage in new, more productive activities which initially feel uncomfortable.

More than anything else, this endemic human trait limits all we're capable of being. All growth, whether individual or collective (from organisations to nations), to the evolution of our species itself, exists outside established comfort zones.

You might not initially be comfortable with the idea of prioritising your own self-development above your business. You might even question its validity. That's perfectly okay. I've been in this business a long time, and I'd expect nothing less of those who come to these ideas for the first time.

Sometimes this 180-degree shift in how you go about business and life disturbs people. Often, the idea of going within to engage and master the non-physical side of our nature is profoundly uncomfortable. If you find yourself disturbed at some level, be assured: it's natural and reasonable to feel that way. I did at one point in my life. So did many of the thousands of entrepreneurs I've led through this journey so far.

Should you experience any doubt, worry, scepticism, or any level of discomfort now or when we collaborate in future, allow me to remind you of the position I took at the beginning of this book: I'm not asking you trust me, I'm asking you to test me.

Developing the owner not the business is not for the faint-hearted—yet I can assure you: no other activity will have such a profound impact on your personal and professional success. This is what makes it the ultimate entrepreneurial success strategy.

As I mentioned earlier, thinking without action is pointless. Yet action without thinking—which is how many business owners go about their day-to-day lives—is disastrous.

Highly successful entrepreneurs get the results they do because at some point in the past they've chosen to think and act differently to the underachieving masses. They became aware of the need to no longer conform, to no longer do what we're programmed to do at a young age, to no longer "follow the crowd".

The most successful business owners became aware of the need to unlearn the unproductive, self-limiting, habitual ways of thinking which stifle potential and constrain the growth of their business. They learned to develop the owner—not the business.

Thinking Like a Highly Successful Person

Highly successful people set different priorities from most people. They know themselves to be the cause of their effects, and so prioritise self-improvement, personal growth, and time to think into their personal and professional results. Most people don't.

It's crucial I elaborate on this term "thinking" because referenced as it normally is, it falls way short of what I'm referring to. And given thinking is the highest function of which we're capable, I don't believe there's a more important subject to understand and master. Many people consider themselves to be thinking just because they're experiencing mental activity—and yet there's a big difference between mental activity and genuinely thinking.

> **"The quality of a person's life is always in direct proportion to the quality of questions they're willing to ask themselves or be asked by another."**

We think in two ways: inductively and deductively. Inductive thinking happens from the inside out, drawing from the untapped potential and wisdom within us. Deductive thinking comes from the outside in. It's how we comprehend and interpret the world around us.

Our upbringing and education system has programmed us to habitually think deductively rather than inductively. Like physical muscles, which weaken and shrink when not used regularly, the psychological "muscles" of our inductive thinking are significantly weaker than those of deductive reasoning.

This is why so many people fail to realise their potential. All potential lies within, not outside of us. All that exists outside of us is opportunity.

Inductive thinking is the process of going within. It draws insight ("in" sight—an inner eye of understanding) from creative resources, far greater than our intellect, deep within us all. Yet we spend most of our lives unconscious of it. This source of creativity feeds you with ideas, reveals solutions to existing challenges and, if engaged appropriately, creates the

51

future through visioning or, as Walt Disney referred to it, "Imagineering".

How To Transform The Quality Of Your Thinking

The quality of a person's life is always in direct proportion to the quality of questions they're willing to ask themselves or be asked by another. Searching, inquisitive questions prompt deep thinking—a "secret" to success known only too well to the Ancient Greek philosopher Socrates, who wisely announced, "I cannot teach anybody anything. I can only make them think."

No one has to think when they're told what to think. We massively underestimate the power of questions, and we massively overestimate the power of information.

We're significantly psychologically handicapped and therefore limited because we're not raised to ask ourselves enough of the kinds of question challenging and stretching us to elevate our consciousness.

Think about it. Since you were first *compos mentis*, you've pretty much been told what to do and what to think.

In the early years, it kept us out of danger. Quite rightly, our parents and guardians told us not to put cutlery in the electrical outlet, to not touch the hot pan or the sharp knife, because we'd come to harm. As infants, we're ignorant to the perils of the physical world, so our survival relies on our guardians telling us what to do and what not to do. However, once we're at an age where we're competent at staying alive, we require a different approach.

> **"Nature hasn't limited us, nurture has."**

It's not the approach most of us experience—not because our parents didn't love us or want the best for us; they just didn't know any better. They can't give what they never had. They did the best they could given their own experience and the awareness coming from it.

The problem is, as the mind evolves and matures, the engagement model doesn't. It never adapts. As we enter mainstream education, teachers pour endless amounts of data and information into our minds in the hope we can recall it in future when a test or exam requires it of us.

> **"The word education comes from the Latin word *educo*, meaning to draw from within."**

I'm not suggesting people don't think and learn within this form of so-called education—however, I can assure you it doesn't require or evoke inductive thinking, and it doesn't unlock untapped potential.

The traditional education system is barely an education system at all. In the main, it's an information system which trains and programs its participants only to think deductively. At no point are we led to pursue self-knowledge curiously, to ask ourselves powerful questions to draw answers from the deep, untapped resources residing within each of us.

Nothing stifles us more. Nature hasn't limited us, nurture has. Our nature is limitless.

Understand this: the word education comes from the Latin word *educo*, meaning "to draw from within". It doesn't mean memorising facts and repeating them sometime in the future. The traditional education system would be so much more effective if its purpose were to ensure by the time its participants enter the commercial world, they'd have an unquenchable thirst for self-knowledge, and be imbued with a lifelong desire to pursue it.

Improving how you think doesn't happen on its own. It's not automatic. Getting fitter in mind is like getting fitter in the body: you have to work at it. That said, nothing will reward you more exponentially, because everything you experience begins (and ends) with the mind.

If you're willing to engage the most creative tool you'll ever have at your disposal, you'll unleash a level of creativity into your life you never previously dreamed of. You'll become far more resourceful, far more successful at solving problems, far better at overcoming challenges, and far more skilled at recognising and creating opportunities.

Imagine the consequences for your business. Imagine the implications for your life. Both will be transformed, continuously, for the better. Ever-increasing profits, personal prosperity, wealth, health, happiness, wellbeing, and freedom are direct consequences of raising your consciousness to improve the quality of thinking you bring to your life.

The Power of Habit

What I'm about to reveal may surprise you. It's extremely likely, for most of the time, you're not conscious in the act of creating your life experience. We're all guilty of thinking habitually, operating as if on autopilot, with little or no thought applied to the results we're generating.

This is often referred to as "learned behaviour".

In fact, one paper published by a Duke University

researcher in 2006 found more than 40% of the actions we perform daily are habits, not decisions. In my experience, it's much higher.

In certain situations, learned behaviours serve us well. For example, we no longer have to think through the process of how to open a door. When you were a toddler, you had no idea how to get past the giant obstacle filling the hole in the wall between two rooms.

Back then you'd have to consciously focus on how to do it until, one day, you didn't need to think at all— **"Unconscious living is the source of our problems."** you just opened the door while your conscious mind focused on other, less mundane matters. Opening the door became a learned behaviour. In other words, you performed the act automatically... or to be more precise, unconsciously.

If you drive, cast your mind back to when you first got behind the wheel of a car. If your experience was anything like mine, you didn't have a clue and were way outside your comfort zone. For a start, assuming you learned to drive in a manual transmission vehicle as I did, there's the three pedals and two legs ratio. Then we had to monitor speed and calculate braking distance, decide when to shift gears, use indicators, notice traffic and pedestrians, use rear-view and side mirrors, hand brakes, and everything else keeping us from being a potential danger to ourselves and others.

In those first few lessons behind the wheel, you were consciously incompetent: you knew you didn't know how to drive. Today, you're an unconscious competent. You don't think about any of it—it just gets done. Through a process of spaced repetition (driving lessons over weeks or months) you've programmed the unconscious part of your personality—where all learning takes place—to produce learned behaviour through your body.

Have you ever been a victim of the so-called "junction thieves"? Have you ever driven down a motorway or freeway and found yourself approaching Junction 13 when you were meant to come off two junctions before at Junction 11—yet you have no recollection of passing the previous exits?

Or maybe you've been on a familiar journey—from home to the office, for example—and when you arrive at your destination, you can't recall any part of your trip. It's certainly happened to me. Such is the degree of how unconscious we are in the act of driving, our conscious mind is free to think into whatever we choose to think about: what's for lunch, the next vacation, our partner naked, or the next strategy meeting with the team.

Becoming unconsciously competent and operating on autopilot in rudimentary activities (like opening doors and driving cars) serves us because it leaves the thinking mind free to focus on more productive pursuits.

However, being unconscious in the rest of our lives doesn't serve us at all. In fact, it's disastrous. Unconscious living is the source of our problems and limitations.

There are always consequences. When we think habitually, we create habitually. We act accordingly and recreate our existing realities over and over again. Being in the habit of believing highly successful entrepreneurs are born with attributes the rest of us just don't have, has consequences—and life will shape up accordingly. Just as it will if you're in the habit of prioritising getting busy in the mechanics of your business rather than improving the quality of thinking you're applying to it.

I'm not suggesting your business can't grow this way. However, its growth will be restricted. You'll only take it so far. Transformational improvements in results do not come from habitual ways of thinking. Inevitably, this leads to an alarming and uncomfortable truth: for the vast majority of our time, we're not thinking into our results. We're not consciously participating in the creation of our outcomes. There lies the ultimate threat to your personal and professional success.

If for most, if not all, of the time you're not conscious of being the creator of your outcomes, and consequently you're not aware in the creative process itself, is it any wonder your results aren't what you'd like them to be?

The antidote to this life-depreciating problem is awareness—developing the habit of thinking about what you're thinking about... and the consequences.

I'll elaborate on this in greater detail in the next chapter. For now, remember this: greater success, in any aspect of life, is merely a process of continually modifying or replacing habits no longer serving you in the pursuit of your goals, dreams, and aspirations, with practices that do.

However, you first need to become aware of the habits no longer serving you. Only then can you evaluate, modify and replace them. You'll never think of modifying and replacing something you're not aware of and you'll never look to replace something you're not aware of.

Remember, habits are unconscious, learned behaviours, beneath the radar of your thinking mind, reproduced without the need for conscious intervention. You don't need to think into a habit, it just is. That's why increasing your awareness by raising your consciousness—developing the owner, not the business—is the ultimate entrepreneurial success strategy.

Shift Your Priority To Create The Change You Want

This first Pillar of Mastery is about shifting priorities. The most successful entrepreneurs have very different priorities from perpetually underachieving and struggling business owners. The Top 0.1% do not fight to keep their heads above water. Those who are struggling in business at best accomplish the mediocrity of a comfortable living.

Highly successful entrepreneurs consciously prioritise developing themselves above developing their business, because they understand the business will never outgrow the thinking they bring to it.

Highly successful people self-educate. They understand if they improve how they think, they are their company's greatest asset. Conversely, they also know if they're not improving how they think, they are their company's greatest liability.

So it shouldn't come as any surprise to know successful entrepreneurs are willing to back themselves and continually invest time, money and energy in products, services, and experiences to improve their thinking. They're eager to work to master their minds.

To master the mind, and align both conscious and unconscious, is to master self. To master self is to master life, for you are the creator of your life experience, whether you're aware of or can accept this level of truth, or not. And to master life is to consciously create and live a fulfilled, rewarding, meaningful life on your own terms.

Exceptional entrepreneurs with exceptional results read books like this one. They don't just read it, though, they study it and apply themselves to the questions and implementation strategies within it.

> **"Wise are those who learn that the bottom line doesn't always have to be their top priority."**
> **~ William Arthur Ward**

They invest in self-improvement programmes. They work with mentors. They hire a professional coach to challenge their existing thought processes and help them overcome the self-imposed, limiting beliefs residing just below their conscious awareness keeping them chained to existing results.

They read, listen to, and watch personal success information and model the habits of highly successful people. They are willing to do what most business owners are not willing to do. They're eager to put their money where their potential is.

Learning to develop yourself—the owner, not the business—is the first pillar of mastery, and here's why. To become rich in life, you need first to grow rich in your mind. I'm not sharing anything new here, and perhaps you've heard it before—but whether or not you know this great truth isn't the question, is it? No, the question is: how much do you live it? Because by the end of this book, you'll have a firm understanding of why developing yourself, not your business, must be your life's priority.

Jim Rohn was one of the most successful entrepreneurs of his genre. He was broke at the age of 25 but a millionaire by the time he was 30. He said, "If you work hard on your job, you can make a living—but if you work hard on yourself, you can make a fortune."

He was right... and his results proved it. He also made this telling observation: "Character isn't something you were born with and can't change, like your fingerprints. It's something you weren't born with and must take responsibility for forming."

So few of us take responsibility. And we reap what we sow as a consequence.

An Uncomfortable Truth

Napoleon Hill understood a thing or two about what creates extraordinary success in life. He wrote the now-infamous *Think & Grow Rich*, first published in 1937. His book was the result of two decades of research into the most powerful, influential, and successful people of the time.

We live in a different world from the one Hill experienced back in the first half of the twentieth century. However, for all our technological advances, human nature is fundamentally the same. Despite some language differences, Hill's body of work is as relevant today as it's been at any time since its release.

Think & Grow Rich is credited with creating more millionaires than any other written media. Given Hill's research was sponsored by the business magnate Andrew Carnegie, a billionaire during the early twentieth century, who had sixty millionaires working for him, it's a book worthy of study. Your library isn't complete without it.

In Chapter 2, you'll discover eye-opening and irrefutable scientific research validating everything in this book so far.

However, before we move on, it's vital to reiterate and amplify an irrefutable truth that is, for the overwhelming majority who never make the grade, an uncomfortable truth—yet it's a given to highly successful people:

You are the creator of your outcomes. Nothing is being done to you—all experiences are created *by* you. You are *always* in the process of creation, and you are the cause of all your effects. Even when circumstances outside your control affect you, you're still in complete control of how you react to what happens and what you do next. This truth is the most empowering understanding you will ever grasp.

Only by accepting yourself as the cause of the current conditions and circumstances of your business and personal life can you take responsibility for improving them.

This is an awakening. It's the most crucial step of all in shifting from the mindset of the struggling business owner with an average business producing mediocre returns, or the business owner who focuses exclusively on the bottom line while the rest of life (health, family, relationships, personal growth, etc.) is abandoned or neglected, to the psychology of the high achiever who enjoys extraordinary success—not just in business, but in all aspects of life. As William Arthur Ward wisely observed: "Wise are those who learn that the bottom line doesn't always have to be their top priority."

Instantly this new awareness puts you at the cause, rather than the effect, end of your life. You've always been at the cause end—you just weren't aware of it.

In accepting this great truth, you become a conscious architect of every result in your life, instead of the passive, unconscious spectator lost in the illusion of your life being shaped by forces outside of you.

Many people find this difficult to accept. Such a realisation brings with it too much responsibility, because if you're the creator of the conditions and circumstances of your life—if you're the cause of your effects—there can be no more victims and villains or mysterious, unproven forces such as "luck" to blame. And there can be no deity contradicting the expression of its own laws to shape life on your behalf despite granting you free will. All there is, is the outcome of your thoughts and what's sponsoring them.

The Essential Ingredient

We've now firmly established if you continue to think and act as you have been up to this point, you'll only recreate the results you're currently experiencing.

And when it comes to your career, if you continue to think and act in a similar vein to how most business owners think and act—given the vast majority are struggling, and working harder and harder for longer and longer to achieve abject mediocrity at best—you will only, and can only, create similar results.

> "Life doesn't give you what you want, it gives you who you are."

There is no escaping the flawless expression of cause and effect. As a highly conscious teacher once accurately observed: "By their fruits, you will know them."

The Top 0.1% live at the cause end of the cause and effect equation. They understand life does not give you what you want, it gives you who you are.

James Allen, one of the most celebrated personal success authors of all time, insightfully wrote:

"Circumstance does not make the man; it reveals him to himself." He also said: "Men are anxious to improve circumstances, but never willing to improve themselves—they, therefore, remain bound."

Those words were first published back in 1903, and they're still as profoundly accurate in their assessment of most human beings today as they were back then.

Over the past few decades, detailed research has produced scientifically validated information proving why developing yourself at the level of character—to improve the psychological blueprint creating your results in every aspect of life—is the most important work you'll ever undertake if you're to enjoy a level of success eluding most business owners.

I encourage you to pay close attention, because when it comes to understanding your potential, and what it means for you, your business, your family, and your financial future, I'm about to give you the best news you've heard in a long, long time. But before I do, and before we move onto Chapter 2, let me ask you an important question.

What do you honestly believe about your potential? I've talked a lot about the Top 0.1%... but what about driven, ambitious business owners like you who aspire to join the Top 0.1% and are actively working to make it a reality in their lives?

Elaine Frostman is a business coach, and a long-standing member of my Entrepreneurial Mastery Inner Circle™. She also leads one of the Elite Mastermind™ groups my business provides to growth-centric, ambitious entrepreneurs all over the world.

Here's what she discovered about the cause and effect relationship of her own unconscious programming... and how she took conscious control.

Elaine's Story

The real big lesson for me was having self-belief and questioning some of those self-limiting beliefs. Those were the biggest shifts for me. The First Pillar makes you think about your own programming right from childhood. Working through the First Pillar brought up some things from my education... I didn't attend the best school! I came from a very humble background, a working-class family. Nobody in my family went to university or started their own business.

Mine was a lovely family, but they were very much in the mindset: money is the root of all evil, and you'll never achieve more than you have already achieved.

The First Pillar really did make me think into where my self-limiting beliefs come from. It gave me the ability to work back and reprogram myself with some of the more positive thoughts about myself and my abilities. From there, I was able to start resetting goals and objectives and putting more clarity around them.

Also, having understood where some of these limiting beliefs came from, I found the confidence to be more bold and brave about goals. Instead of asking, "Why?" I started asking, "Why not?" I started thinking bigger. If I set a goal for a certain turnover for the next twelve months, why not double it? Or do it in six months, rather than twelve months.

Thinking Into Results: What Will Your Story Be?

Napoleon Hill said, "No man has a chance to enjoy permanent success until he begins to look in a mirror for the real cause of all his mistakes."

Make no mistake: what you believe about yourself and your potential determines everything in your life. Given what you've discovered in this first chapter, it'd be wise to explore what your truth has been until now. Perhaps you believe there's a limit on your potential. Maybe you think some people have more than others. Or perhaps you believe we're all gifted with unlimited potential seeking expression through our natural talents, gifts and abilities? It's time to find out.

Earlier I shared how success is simply a matter of evaluating, modifying or replacing habits no longer serving you in the pursuit of your desired outcomes with habits that do.

This is your opportunity to make it happen. Remember, the quality of your life will be determined by the quality of question you're willing to be asked. Explorative questions raise awareness, increase consciousness, and improve the quality of your thinking.

Embrace the habit of being asked powerful questions now. They're the key to success. Powerful questions are how you fully engage the astonishing creative abilities of your mind. They're how you unlock the untapped potential within you because powerful coaching questions make the unconscious conscious.

The only reason you've not expressed your untapped potential until this point in your life is you're not currently consciously aware of it.

Invest your time wisely and reflect on the three questions below. Remember, old habits die hard, so make a conscious decision to not move on to the next chapter without thinking into these questions first. I promise you, this habit will reward you for the rest of your life.

WARNING: Do not proceed to Chapter 2 yet!

Before you read on, make sure you download the free Success Implementation Guide™ (SIG) accompanying this book. The coaching resources within the SIG™ ensure the transformational benefits of the tried, tested, and proven strategies you've discovered so far are put to work in your business and professional life.

Should you proceed to Chapter 2 without engaging the questions in the SIG™, you will not internalise and grasp the powerful success principles of this chapter.

Do not make the grave error of convincing yourself you'll return to the resources later. Invariably, despite best intentions, it doesn't happen. I know, because I made the same mistake for many years—and it comes with a heavy price. Learn from my mistakes, apply yourself to the coaching questions immediately and, I can assure you, you'll reap the rewards.

christian-simpson.com/ult-sig

Chapter 2

The Intelligence Myth

"The function of education is to teach one to think intensively and to think critically. Intelligence plus character—that is the goal of true education."

Martin Luther King

Maths just didn't make sense to me. I once did an IQ test, and the questions seemed absurd. For years I hadn't been able to work out the difference between gross and net," said one of the most successful entrepreneurs the world has ever seen.

"I'd probably fail school exams if I took them today. I never quite mastered my times-tables and remembering and regurgitating lots of facts and figures, and getting them on paper quickly for exams, was a nightmare.

"This isn't how people are assessed in the real world, so why do we do this in school?" he asks.

The businessman I'm quoting is Sir Richard Branson.

At school, his teachers labelled him "dumb"

because of his dyslexia. He never excelled academically, and he dropped out of school aged sixteen. Yet despite these so-called "handicaps", Branson went on to make his fortune by building the Virgin Group, one of the most diverse and successful collectives of enterprises on the planet.

He's not the only school dropout to excel in business and in life—so perhaps society ought to rethink what "intelligence" means, and how it contributes to success.

By the time we're beyond the playful, creative pursuits of kindergarten and nursery, and into primary-level education, the importance of intellectual intelligence and academic prowess is drummed into us.

At the time of writing, the UK education system starts subjecting children to examinations at the age of six and seven. It's barbaric, horrific, and driven purely as a vote winner by self-serving politicians seeking to convince the electorate of the merits of flawed educational policies. I digress. The point is, from a very early age, we're programmed to benchmark ourselves by our intellectual ability alone.

We must be academically smart.

We must pass exams.

We must conform.

There is some excellent news, however, particularly if you struggled at school (and I didn't exactly set the world alight). This model of assessing intelligence and potential is not only archaic, outdated and extremely limiting—it's also flawed.

IQ isn't everything. In fact, it's nowhere near it.

Decades of research by the Toronto-based company Multi-Health Systems have shown IQ contributes somewhere between 1% and 20% to success in today's business environment.

Whether your IQ contributes 19% or 2% depends on the nature of your work. If you're in highly analytical work, like a scientist or financial analyst, your IQ will contribute closer to 20% to your success. If you're not, it's much, much less. On average, IQ contributes just 6% to success in today's business environment. Its influence on success—not just in business, but in life itself—is grossly over-inflated. The British philosopher, logician, mathematician, and historian Bertrand Russell didn't have this research to hand during his lifetime, but it didn't prevent him from accurately assessing the problem: "Men are born ignorant not stupid; they are made stupid by education."

Now stay with me here, because the news keeps getting better and better. If you're serious about enjoying the kind of personal and professional success most business owners never see, this is where the rubber meets the road.

What A Three-Figure IQ Really Means

First, for context, a reminder: you and I are products of our environment. We all are. And if you were educated in the Western world, your intelligence, capabilities, and potential were assessed by your intellectual quotient— your IQ. You probably had an IQ test at some point in the past. Perhaps you've even taken one recently. Maybe you remember your score.

The average IQ is said to be 100, and it's a measure of your intellectual, analytical, logical, and rational abilities.

The underlying assumption of the current education

system, and, in no small degree of society as a whole, is if you have a three-figure IQ, you're well equipped for success in life.

If you don't, they say, it's likely you'll struggle. That's a lie. It's simply not true. Not when it comes to the attributes you need to enjoy a highly successful life. And not when it comes to making the health, wealth, prosperity and freedom of the entrepreneurial dream a reality in your life.

A three-figure IQ equips you for success in academia. Academia rewards you for what you know. Life outside academia rewards you for what you do.

As the American author Tom Bodett put it perfectly: "In school, you're taught a lesson and then given a test. In life, you're given a test that teaches you a lesson."

The history books are full of brilliant men and women who were dismal failures in the classroom and the world's full of them today too. Richard Branson, whom I mentioned earlier, is probably the most publicised example of all. Remember the highly successful entrepreneur I referred to at the start of Chapter 1? The one who'd generated more than ten million dollars from scratch in the first year of trading in just one of his businesses? He's a high school dropout—written off by teachers, friends and, sadly, family alike.

You probably know someone who's incredibly bright intellectually—a real brain-box—but for some reason, they just can't seem to cut it in the commercial world.

There's a multitude of people with an alphabet of letters after their name who just can't cut the mustard, and many of them never understand why.

Knowledge certainly has its place, but if knowledge

was all it took to be successful every member of MENSA would be at the top of the socio-economic pyramid—and they're not.

School Smart Or Street Smart?

If you were able to assemble all your fellow students from your school days, you're likely to discover a very interesting and illuminating commonality.

> "Academia rewards you for what you know. Life outside of academia rewards you for what you do."

Those often referred to as "school smarts", who had the monopoly on the A-grades, will generally be far less successful than the "street smarts"—the kids who just scraped by in the classroom, yet were popular in the playground. According to conventional perspectives and academic success indicators, the street-smart kids probably weren't going to amount to much in life. Yet today, you'll find many of them are successful business owners, or board members of large corporations, or doing something similarly impressive.

So what does this have to do with you and your business success? The answer is *everything*.

Your intelligence goes way beyond just your intellect alone. There are four components to your overall intelligence. IQ is only one of them, and it's the least influential in terms of success. I'm not suggesting it's not important, I'm merely pointing out it's nowhere near as important as we're led to believe. You wouldn't be reading this book if you didn't believe you were capable of achieving more than you currently are.

You want better results in your life—more wealth, prosperity, and freedom. And why not? After all, you've taken all the risks. You've put in the hard, sometimes painful, work. If the rewards aren't forthcoming—as is the case for the vast majority of business owners—what's the point? It's not only okay to desire more, but it's also perfectly natural you should. As the Victorian author James Allen observed, "Man is a growth by law and not a creation by artifice."

I've had the privilege of spending many years, and thousands of hours, coaching people to much greater success in their lives. This wealth of experience has proven to me, over and over again, there is more potential locked up inside each and every one of us than we can possibly imagine. Welcome to the truth of you. Whether you choose to accept it or not is your business. Either way, you'll live the consequences. It's vital to stress it's not your IQ determining how much of your untapped potential is expressed into your life, it's how advanced and mature the four aspects of your intelligence are.

The evidence to support this conclusion is overwhelming, revealed by years observing the astonishing transformations in the lives of those I serve. Throughout *The 4 Pillars of Mastery*™ books and the vital resources they contain, I'll prove it to you.

There Is Much More To You Than You Think

Intelligence is not just about one single component. And if it were, as I'm about to reveal, it most certainly wouldn't be your IQ.

You are a three-fold being. You have a body. Most people live as if they are the body—you have a body, but you are not your body. You have a mind—the most powerful, creative tool humanity will ever know—

which, sadly, is forgotten, abandoned, and neglected by most people. And you are consciousness, the "ghost in the machine", the life force within it all. Body, mind, and spirit, as some like to call it. This trinity reveals how you simultaneously operate on three planes of existence.

You have four components to your intelligence. The interplay between this broader spectrum of intelligences determines how much of the unexpressed potentiality within you finds its way into your results.

The four components are as follows:
1. Intellectual quotient—the familiar IQ.
2. Emotional intelligence—often referred to as EQ.
3. Spiritual intelligence—known as SQ.
4. Physical intelligence—or PQ.

Having discussed IQ as a measure of human intelligence, what constitutes the other three?

An entire book could be dedicated to each of the components of intelligence I'm about to outline, and numerous books do.

However, the purpose of this book is to introduce you to a much broader understanding of your capabilities, so you grasp why *Develop The Owner, Not The Business* is irrefutably the ultimate entrepreneurial success strategy and should be a priority in your life. Here's a brief overview of what you need to know.

Emotional Intelligence (EQ)

Emotional intelligence is a series of emotional and social skills influencing how we perceive and express ourselves, how we cope with challenges, how we develop and maintain social relationships, and how we use emotional information effectively and meaningfully.

It includes emotional awareness, the ability to use emotions during tasks like problem-solving, and the ability to manage emotions—including regulating your own feelings and influencing the mood of others.

For example, EQ enables us to modify a reaction—which is an automatic behaviour occurring without conscious intervention—to a response, which is preceded by thought. In other words, emotional intelligence gives you conscious control in any given experience.

Spiritual Intelligence (SQ)

The first thing to establish about spiritual intelligence is what it isn't. Spiritual intelligence is not a theology, it's not a religion, and it isn't religious. It's also not a moral code or a framework of ethics—yet spiritual intelligence may feed all these things.

Your spiritual intelligence is an inherent, organic attribute of your being. It's the natural existential "life force" at the core of you, the seeker of growth and fuller expression through you.

Spiritual intelligence is the seat of your potential. It drives you to become more than you are, so you may be, do, have, and give more. How much of your SQ is expressed into your results is determined by your level of consciousness. Your spiritual intelligence needs no development; you do, as the vehicle through which your SQ is expressed—which is the purpose of not only this book and the whole *4 Pillars of Mastery*™ series, it's the primary focus of my body of work.

Physical Intelligence (PQ)

While the focus of this book and its resources is the

non-physical side of your personality, I'd be negligent in my duty if I didn't offer some insight into the inherent intelligence at work within your physical body, too. You might be wondering how our physical bodies can be "intelligent"—so let me explain with a story about my son, Jacob.

In 2004, Jacob had a febrile convulsion. He was an infant at the time, he was fighting an infection, and consequently, his body temperature was high.

We were upstairs in my home office when it happened. I was holding Jacob in my arms to comfort him when, all of a sudden, as I looked into his big blue eyes, I sensed something was wrong—as if he'd been "reset". For a second, his eyes were static, dead central, almost... lifeless and then, alarmingly, I watched his eyes move slowly toward his eyelashes, and roll to the back of his head.

Instantly, driven by primal parental instinct, I'd charged down the stairs, crashed through two child-safety stair gates (removing huge chunks of plaster from the walls in the process), got in my car (leaving the front door wide open), and sped to the doctor's surgery... with a limp, lifeless Jacob still in my arms.

All kinds of terrifying ideas sprang into my consciousness. I thought I was losing my son. I thought he'd be more brain damaged with each passing second. None of this was true, but I didn't know it at the time. As I eventually discovered, Jacob's body temperature had gone beyond an acceptable threshold. Infants cannot regulate their body temperature like adults can.

He was already running a temperature, and when he was in my arms, I was adding my body heat to the equation. I didn't determine the threshold, neither did

Jacob; the intelligence at play in Jacob's cells did. His physical intelligence stepped in to protect his body from overheating to the point of harm.

Your body is a community of cells. Scientists estimate the average human body has 37.2 trillion cells. Each of those cells has intelligence, and it not only enables cells to communicate with other cells; it also informs the entire organism and the brain via the nervous system.

When faced with certain, life-threatening conditions, this inherent intelligence can and will override conscious control—hence why people "pass out" and slip into comas.

There are literally billions of processes underway in your body as you read this sentence. Cells are dividing, dying, being recycled, getting cleansed of waste, you're digesting your last meal, firing neurons in your brain, beating your heart... all of which is just a fraction of what's going on. Here's the point: you're not consciously doing *any* of it, although you are doing *all* of it. The life force within you, the one you're not fully conscious of, is doing it all for you, simultaneously, with astounding precision.

Aside from inherent auto-responses like the one I described above, cells respond to their environment. In other words, we're not powerless biochemical machines. Our beliefs, the thoughts they generate, the emotional consequences of those thoughts, and the actions they ultimately produce all significantly influence the health and function of the cells within your body.

Character, Potential, And Results

Now a far more comprehensive understanding of

the depth and breadth of human intelligence has been established, it's important to understand your character is a result of the combination and interplay between the broader components of your intelligence.

Remember, how much of your untapped potential is expressed into your results depends on the maturity and cohesion between all aspects of your intelligence. This understanding alone is the all-important first step to mastery.

To give some context to my previous comment, and to show how emotional and spiritual intelligence has a much more significant influence on results than IQ alone, consider this: a study conducted at the

> **"Things have to change *in* you for things to change *for* you."**

University of Pennsylvania found some students who didn't have the highest IQs in their peer group still achieved high grades.

They might not have been book smarts, but they had something else. They had grit. The Oxford dictionary describes grit as "courage and resolve; strength of character". The Merriam-Webster dictionary defines it as "firmness of character; indomitable spirit".

Grit is less about intellectual prowess or cognitive ability, it's about cognitive control—your ability to delay gratification and persevere, despite setbacks, in the pursuit of your goal. It's about focus, courage, a ruthless determination to succeed, an unwavering commitment to learning, and the ability to manage and control any emotionally charged reaction putting the successful attainment of the goal at risk.

And here's the fascinating part for those of us who don't have genius IQ scores: a thirty-year study of more than a thousand children found cognitive control—grit—was a better predictor of success than a child's IQ... and a better predictor of success than their family's wealth and social status.

In other words, focusing on maturing the inherent intelligences of character is great for business and fundamental to your success in every other aspect of life. Can the evidence to support why developing the owner not the business is the ultimate entrepreneurial success strategy be more compelling?

Here's a truth you simply can't afford to ignore any longer: things have to change *in* you for things to change *for* you. When you understand yourself better, when you start to develop yourself in areas you've not been raised or programmed to develop, your results, in every aspect of your life, will improve immeasurably. And this is why what's about to be revealed in Chapter 3 is so important to you as you continue to discover the truth about what creates outstanding entrepreneurial success. Here's how one of my clients, Florin Lungu, discovered how things have to change *in* you for things to change *for* you.

Florin's Story

When I first signed up for Pillar 1, in video format, I didn't actually do the work in the way I was supposed to. I had the Success Implementation Guide™ [which contains the all-important coaching resources to ensure the ultimate entrepreneurial success strategy is put to work in your business and personal life], and I was thinking I'd just listen to the Four Pillars and watch the videos and get what I needed. I didn't take it as seriously as I should have, so not much changed for me.

Intellectually, I grasped the ideas and understood that I'm the cause of all my effects and I need to invest in myself... but it wasn't until I took the Success Implementation Guide™ and applied the process as I should, that I really realised I'm the cause of all the effects in my life. So I stopped blaming someone else—and I think this is the biggest shift that happened in my mindset. I realised I am responsible for everything I have in my life.

> **"If you fail to go within, you will go without."**

When I stopped saying, "I don't have time" or "My wife doesn't support me" or "Sweden is difficult, and I don't know the language"... that's when everything started to change.

Thinking Into Results: What Will Your Story Be?

Like Florin, most people avoid the most critical step of all. We've all been programmed to operate this way by the model of "learning" we were subjected to at school. Consequently, we operate under the same flawed premise all our lives. We gather information—read something, watch something, listen to a speech, lecture or presentation, just like we did in the classroom—and expect our results to improve accordingly. We're all guilty of it.

Even those of us who become aware of its limitations easily backslide into the deeply entrenched, habitual behaviours ingrained from years of being programmed to "learn" in a certain way. We all find something interesting and think it'll be enough to simply read it, despite a plethora of evidence from life experience telling us otherwise.

There's been a lot of ground covered in this last chapter, so before moving on to the next chapter, invest your time wisely by capturing and internalising the powerful and proven ideas you're now being exposed to. Remember: intellectual comprehension of this information will change nothing. Internalise these ideas by addressing the coaching questions found in the book and the downloadable Success Implementation Guide™. This is the process by which you raise your consciousness, modify your beliefs, improve the quality of your thinking, alter your behaviour and, consequently, generate improved results in your life.

Until you go within, to think into what's sponsoring the thoughts, feelings, and actions creating your existing reality, very little, if anything, will improve.

If you fail to go within, you will go without. What you're seeking is wisdom, not knowledge. Wisdom is knowledge applied through an evaluated experience— hence why the explorative power of coaching questions is so vital to success.

In the next chapter, I'll share further insight, backed by decades of scientific research, into the limitless potential lying dormant within you... and, most importantly, how you call it forth and express it into your personal and professional results.

One final point: I do not use terms such as "limitless potential" lightly. I'm very aware of the gravity of the statement. Such phrases are often overused and thrown about cheaply without little to no substance behind them. This chapter, and those following will continue to buck the trend, ensuring you're equipped not just with knowledge, but with wisdom—the inner eye of understanding—the essential step if you're to become all you're capable of becoming—not just as an entrepreneur, but as a human being. On that note, I'll leave you to address the following questions:

- What are your most prominent revelations from this last chapter?
- What has changed for you as a consequence?
- What will change for you as a consequence of your new understanding?
- What are the immediate steps you need to take?

Download and use your Success Implementation Guide™ to think into and write down your answers to the questions. Remember: writing deepens thinking, and improved thinking improves results.

WARNING: Do not proceed to Chapter 3 yet!

Before you read on, make sure you download the free Success Implementation Guide™ (SIG) accompanying this book. The coaching resources within the SIG™ ensure the transformational benefits of the tried, tested, and proven strategies you've discovered so far are put to work in your business and professional life.

Should you proceed to Chapter 3 without engaging the questions in the SIG™, you will not internalise and grasp the powerful success principles of this chapter.

Do not make the grave error of convincing yourself you'll return to the resources later. Invariably, despite best intentions, it doesn't happen. I know, because I made the same mistake for many years—and it comes with a heavy price. Learn from my mistakes, apply yourself to the coaching questions immediately and, I can assure you, you'll reap the rewards.

christian-simpson.com/ult-sig

Chapter 3

Uncharted Waters: The Undiscovered Self

"What lies behind us, and what lies before us, are tiny matters compared to what lies within us."

Ralph Waldo Emerson

Sitting in a stunning position on the south-west slope of Mount Parnassus in Greece, lies the ancient sanctuary of Delphi. According to the Greek writer Pausanias, the Temple of Apollo at Delphi had the Ancient Greek aphorism "know thyself" inscribed in the pronaos (forecourt).

Later, Ancient Greek philosophers elaborated further on the wisdom of the inscription, including Socrates, who at his own trial, said: "The unexamined life is not worth living." How true. And how typical it remains, over two thousand years later, for human beings to live "an unexamined life". The fundamental message at the heart of this book is not new. The ultimate entrepreneurial success strategy—develop the owner, not the business—is merely an entrepreneurial take on the age-old wisdom shared by a myriad of teachers over a multitude of generations. For example, another Greek philosopher and scientist, Aristotle, said, "Knowing yourself is the beginning of all wisdom."

The oldest book in the world is the *Tao Te Ching*, written by Lao-Tzu. In it, he wrote: "Knowing others is intelligence; knowing yourself is true wisdom. Mastering others is strength; mastering yourself is true power. If you realise that you have enough, you are truly rich."

> **"Knowing yourself is the beginning of all wisdom."**
> **~ Aristotle**

According to historians, in Ancient Egypt, there were two parts of the ancient Luxor Temple: the External Temple, where "beginners" were allowed to enter, and the Internal Temple, where only those who'd proven worthy and ready to acquire more knowledge and insights were permitted to enter.

I operate from the same premise at every level of my business (from assessing the current psychological profile of business owners with the Entrepreneurial Wealth Scorecard™ to the thorough application process of The Elite Mastermind™), so it appears I'm simply adopting an age-old practice.

There are many insightful proverbs on both the External and Internal Temples of Luxor speaking into the importance of self-discovery and self-mastery.

For example, on the external temple, it says, "The kingdom of Heaven is already within you; if you understand yourself you will find it." Be careful of misinterpreting this message because of religious programming; the kingdom of heaven is not a destination, it's a state of consciousness.

Within the inner temple, one of the many proverbs is, "Man, know thyself, and you are going to know the gods." Again, do not view this through the lens of religion or mythology. In "knowing the gods" it again refers to higher levels of consciousness. As the highly conscious teacher known as Christ put it perfectly: "You are gods; and all of you are children of the most high."

The more conscious you become, the higher your self-awareness. The more self-aware you are, in any aspect of life, the better results you'll produce. Our results are always in direct proportion to the level of consciousness we're expressing.

Self-awareness underpins the combining of all aspects of your intelligence. The more self-aware you become (in other words, the more conscious you are), the more mature your innate emotional and spiritual intelligence becomes—leading to ever-increasing alignment across all aspects of your intelligence.

The more mature and aligned your intelligences are, the more of the untapped potential lying dormant within you is expressed through your natural gifts and talent—and the greater success you'll experience in every area of your life. This is why *The 4 Pillars of Mastery*™ books, resources, and all following them, are so imperative to you shaping a fulfilled, prosperous, and meaningful life on your own terms. And it's why, in just a few short years, these powerful strategies have transformed the lives of entrepreneurs in over 160 countries.

Know Thyself

Here's the last thing you might expect someone in my field of expertise to say: there is no potential in your business. There is no potential in your product or service either. There is no potential in your target market audience or the marketplace as a whole. None of the above offer any potential. They offer the opportunity to express potential.

All potential lies within you. Your business, proposition, audience, and marketplace bring you an ever-increasing opportunity to express more potential. The more conscious you become of potential you're currently unconscious of, the more you'll express it into the opportunities life brings your way.

Here's why it's so crucial for you to grasp this: beliefs drive behaviour. And behaviour drives results.

What you believe about your potential will determine whether or not you're willing to go within to discover it. And if you're not willing to go within and find it, you'll never see it expressed into your results.

Your existing results are not a reflection of your potential—your existing results are a reflection of your current awareness of your potential. There's a huge difference in understanding between those two statements. How aware you are of your potential determines how much of it is expressed into your results. You cannot express what you're not aware of. Awareness is everything.

> **"Beliefs drive behaviour. And behaviour drives results."**

I'd like you to consider, for a moment, what could happen…

- If you focused on your current and future potential, not historical performance?
- If you worked on the causes—not the effects— of your results?

- If you began to steer your business from an entirely different perspective?

If all this sounds like abstract theory, I'll use a simple analogy. Have you ever accidentally tapped a button on your smartphone, only to set off something weird and wonderful?

Like switching on a feature you never knew existed? Or finding an app to solve a problem you thought was unsolvable (or a problem you didn't even know you had yet)? And

> **"Your existing results are not a reflection of your potential—your existing results are a reflection of your current awareness of your potential."**

you thought to yourself, "Wow! I didn't know it could do that!"

Of course you didn't know. You were ignorant of the capability because no-one ever showed you it was there. The potential was always there, inside the phone, waiting to be revealed—you weren't consciously aware of it. Your mind is no different. It's filled with deep reservoirs of untapped potential, ready and waiting to be accessed and put to work in your business and personal life—if you know how, and where, to look. For those who don't know how and where to look, a life of underachievement and unfulfillment is inevitable.

The mind is mostly forgotten by the end of academia. In most cases, by the time people reach their thirties, the most creative tool we'll ever know, and the source of our entire life experience, is laid to waste and abandoned.

The mind isn't expanded, nourished or awakened. Instead, it's starved of new and qualitative input, and lulled and dulled by a plethora of distractions designed to avoid the need to think—video games, movies, television, drugs, alcohol.

Very few people read anything of substance anymore—certainly not anything like this book, from which they can learn, grow, and evolve. Most people who can read don't read at all, which gives them no advantage over those who can't. Only a small minority of people write, not as authors of books but as conscious stewards and authors of their own thoughts and emotions. Writing causes thinking—the highest function of which we're capable, and the very activity most humans run from.

Here's another analogy for you: imagine a high-performance sports car. Now imagine it has consciousness—like the cartoon depictions in the Disney movie *Cars*.

Now imagine the car with consciousness knows it has an engine but doesn't know it has more than one gear. Despite all the power under the hood, the vehicle's performance will be chronically limited.

This accurately reveals how most human beings live. Most of us live only as a single-faceted being—a body. A much smaller minority understand themselves to be a body and a mind and actively engage both components. And yet even those of us who engage the mind have only scratched the surface regarding its capabilities.

I met Steve at a marketing seminar in London. You didn't need long in conversation with Steve to know he was intellectually bright—almost too intellectually intelligent for his own good. Steve sat next to me, furiously writing notes. During the breaks, we chatted, and I got to know a reasonable amount about Steve, his business, and his history. Steve had the right work ethic. He had the best intentions, backed up by determination and ambition. Unsurprisingly he exceeded in academia and, from what I could deduce from our conversations, he wasn't shy of rolling his sleeves up. This guy gave me the impression he'd work until he bled.

Steve had all the technical skills he needed to serve his clients and, from what I could gather, he served his clients exceptionally well. You'd think he had a "full house" when it comes to being an entrepreneurial superstar.

Sadly, not. As much as I admired Steve's spirit, and enjoyed his thinly disguised excitement at becoming exposed to the latest tools, techniques and "ninja tactics" the marketing guru

> **"You cannot generate results beyond your present consciousness. You can, however, increase your consciousness."**

shared during the day—I had grave concerns. I knew unless something significant changed in Steve, he was destined to work harder and harder, for longer and longer, for ever diminishing returns.

He was on borrowed time. Steve's failure was inevitable—and yet it wasn't his fault. He didn't know any better. My initial concerns were validated later when I noticed Steve's results from his Entrepreneurial Wealth Scorecard™ (EWS) pop up in my inbox. Steve scored eight on the scorecard.

Despite his intellectual prowess and academic achievement, and despite his admirable worth ethic, technical ability and client-centric approach, Steve's level of consciousness—his awareness—wasn't at the level it needs to be to make his most significant aspirations a reality.

His score revealed his consciousness moves between

the follow-the-crowd psychology of mass consciousness, and aspirational consciousness to be, do and have more. The latter got Steve to the seminar. The former will prevent him from putting what he discovered at the seminar to work to the degree he needs if he's to generate much greater success in life. You cannot generate results beyond your present consciousness. You can, however, increase your consciousness.

I need to check in with you because I'm mindful I'm taking you on quite a journey here. You might not be familiar with terms like "consciousness" and "awareness", at least not concerning how they're the ultimate determinants of your results.

How are you doing? It's important I let you know it's okay if some of this seems somewhat foreign, confusing, mind-boggling or even disturbing at this juncture. In fact, it's perfectly natural if it is. Very few people are exposed to self-knowledge information or teachings in childhood. We've already established you don't find self-knowledge and self-improvement in the academic curriculums of mainstream, adult or business education—so is it any surprise most adults never discover it at all?

I didn't create this body of work to dance around the edges or give just a shallow, surface-level introduction to what makes the Top 0.1% as successful as they are.

I also didn't bring this information to you to read only once and never refer to again. You never graduate from the self-discovery of self-improvement. There will always be much more to the *you* you're consciously aware of, and you'll never exhaust the limitless potential within you. The only thing worse than not reading a good book is only reading it once, so come back to this book time and time again.

The content won't change of course. However, you will. With every read and with every coaching question addressed in your Success Implementation Guide™, your consciousness is elevated, and you'll discover something in the content you couldn't grasp before—because you were not previously at a level of awareness to receive it.

> **"Learning to unlearn is the highest form of learning."**

This is the process by which you make the unconscious conscious, modify your beliefs, and unlearn the habitual ways of thinking which have held you back and undermined your ability to enjoy much greater success in your life.

As Jacqueline E. Purcell observed: "You must unlearn what you have been programmed to believe since birth. That software no longer serves you if you want to live in a world where all things are possible."

It's no coincidence so many entrepreneurial giants are college dropouts and academic failures. It's also no coincidence they're the ones who "modified their programming" and started thinking differently. They may not have been "smart" enough to be top of the class in academia, yet clearly, by their results, they're smart enough to be top of the class in the commercial world. And here's where they got smartest of all: they refused to conform to the norm. They refused to accept convention. The phrase "it's always been done this way" is interpreted as a challenge not a directive by high-achieving business owners.

Believe me, I've witnessed this first hand. I've worked up close with the big hitters. Yes, they see the world through different eyes, and yes, they think and do things very differently as a consequence—disrupting established norms and conventions—yet it's a complete myth they were born this way.

They've been willing to unlearn and relearn. They've undone their environmental programming and adopted a new worldview, just like you are right now by reading these words and embracing the proven resources at your disposal. And, like the big hitters, if you make unlearning and relearning a habit, and you act accordingly to your findings, you'll enjoy whatever outstanding success looks like to you in your life. You have my word on it.

This is a lawful process. It is the cause and effect reality for those who choose to take total responsibility for, and conscious control of, their personal and professional lives. Cause and effect, "the law of laws" as Emerson called it, like all natural laws, will not be denied.

Learning to unlearn is the highest form of learning. As Alvin Toffler eloquently noted: "The illiterate of the future are not those who can't read or write but those who cannot learn, unlearn and relearn."

The Genius Myth

We've already established how our beliefs are the architects of our results. Belief systems are a conglomeration of ideas forming habits, or learned behaviours. Remember, most of the ideas making up your belief systems are not your own—they were inherited from the people around you. Even more concerning is how, despite not being aware of them, for the vast majority of the time (and in some cases, all the time), these unconscious ideas and concepts pull all the strings. It's an unnerving realisation, isn't it? It's unnerving to know you're not often in conscious control of the creative process. Imagine what will happen to your business when you start to take conscious control by putting the ultimate entrepreneurial success strategy, and the remaining *4 Pillars of Mastery™*, to work. Imagine what it will do for your personal life.

To take conscious control of the creative process and create, at will, the results you'd love to have in your personal and professional life, you need **"Life expresses itself through specific natural laws."** to "get under your own hood" and discover how the creative process occurs through the operations of your mind.

So, in the second pillar in *The 4 Pillars of Mastery™* series, I'll share a powerful, life-changing concept bringing you a graphical understanding of your mind and how it produces every result in your life. Visually understanding how you create your reality is a major step in taking control and becoming the fully conscious architect of your results.

For now, though, let's consider consequences. In a previous chapter, I shared detailed research proving IQ isn't anywhere near as influential on our success as we're led to believe.

Most people aren't aware of this research, what it reveals, or its consequences. The vast majority of business owners who remain ignorant to this truth pay a hefty price. Unless the penny drops, and the individual becomes conscious of the cause and effect relationship between the quality of her thinking and results generated in her business and personal life, and until she prioritises self-growth over business development as a consequence of her realisation, life will always reflect her self-imposed limitations. It can do nothing else. Remember, life expresses itself through specific natural laws which never fail to assert themselves and never deviate in their expression.

Now consider this: as we've already established, the vast majority of children are sold a lie—the lie saying their chances of success will be determined, to an enormous degree, by their IQ. In other words, unless they have a high, three-figure IQ, they're probably not going to amount to much beyond average. What a horrible idea to sow deep into the fertile soil of a young person's mind. Remember: when a child is sold a lie by an authority figure in their lives, the child is almost certain to accept it uncritically as truth. In fact, if the child is younger than four years old, it can't do anything else but accept it, because the conscious mind, with its ability to reject or neglect an idea through its reasoning ability, is not yet fully formed.

Most children aren't aware of their IQ assessment until much later in adolescence. However, by this stage, a child has spent many years within the education system. The mind has been heavily programmed, through constant reinforcement and repetition, to be fully receptive to whatever authority figures in the environment say. Consequently, we blindly accept IQ assessment as a credible measurement of our capabilities.

So Johnny buys into the idea there's only so much he can do. He accepts there's a cap on his potential, a lid on his abilities. This idea becomes Johnny's reality. After all, people tend to live up (and down) to the expectations placed upon them—especially expectations from authority figures. Johnny's academic performance follows suit. They get out of Johnny precisely what they predicted they'd get, even though they did more than predict. They *projected*.

Johnny grows up. Now he's Big John in the big commercial world he's so poorly equipped to make a success of himself in. Big John's got big plans. Big John's got a dream. And so Big John starts a business. But Big John is psychologically constrained. He's unconsciously limited, and he doesn't even know it—like Steve who sat next to me in the marketing seminar.

Big John doesn't need to accept the limitation because "little" Johnny unconsciously accepted it for him years before. And now the seed of limitation is a towering tree of fear casting a shadow of doubt over every idea representing growth. It protects its turf by undermining Big John's self-worth. It pollutes his thinking with doubt, worry, fear, and anxiety—and sabotages every act which could lead to vastly improved results. Unless he becomes self-aware enough to become conscious of and separate himself from the belief, to recognise it for what it is—just an idea he accepted uncritically without evaluating its merit—the conditions and circumstances of his life will always reflect the lie he unconsciously holds to be true about his abilities. The lie someone else, who lacked understanding yet was an authoritative source to Johnny, projected into him years before. Now you can understand the insightfulness of Mark Twain's wisdom when he said, "Education consists mainly of what we have unlearned."

Your success is not determined by what you know. It's not about how hard, or how long, you work. It's not about luck, the standard of academic education you received, the state of the economy, what your so-called competitors are doing, the self-serving policymakers and bankers, or whether you were born into wealth or not. Your success—and when I say success, I mean success in every area of your life, not just in business— is determined by one thing and one thing only: how conscious you are in the creation of your outcomes. In other words, the level of consciousness applied to every aspect of your life.

You become more conscious as your self-awareness improves. As you grow more self-aware, your emotional and spiritual intelligence will mature. The more your broader intelligences interact and coordinate, the more unexpressed potential within you is expressed through your natural abilities into your behaviours and results.

The Five Ingredients Of Emotional Intelligence

In Chapter 2, I said a detailed overview of emotional and spiritual intelligence is beyond the scope of this book. While the same premise remains, and spiritual intelligence is a deep and broad topic in and of itself, it's essential to give you further context on why increasing self-awareness and emotional intelligence is vital.

Remember, emotional intelligence is a set of emotional and social skills which influence the way we view and express ourselves. It's how we develop and maintain social relationships, cope with challenges, and use emotional information in a useful and meaningful way. There are five core components of emotional intelligence. Each aspect plays a fundamental role in your success as a business owner. As I highlight each aspect, give serious thought to how it influences your success and be honest with yourself about how you're performing in each area.

1. Self-Perspective

The foundation of emotional intelligence concerns how you view yourself. Becoming more self-aware brings an enhanced ability to identify how you're feeling, why you feel the way you do, and the impact your emotions have on how you, and others, think and act.

Question: How would those closest to you describe your impact on them? Think about your family, friends, colleagues, and professional network. We are continually influencing others, whether we're conscious of it or not.

The question is, do we affect people positively, negatively, or varying degrees of both? And if we became conscious of our influence on others, what could it mean regarding our success?

Would those who know you best describe you as a reactive, or a responsive person?

Then there's your self-image, your ability to recognise your strengths and weaknesses. Being aware of both helps you develop strengths and manage weaknesses far more effectively.

One of the biggest wastes of time, energy and talent is attempting to develop a weakness. We're all gifted in some areas, and not so gifted in others. If you put your back into improving a weakness, you might reach the dizzy heights of being average at it—and given you're reading this book, average is the last thing you intend to be. If you're not gifted in an area, find someone who is and hire them to do it. Don't think about how; think about who. When you find your "who", they'll do the how far better than you ever will. You'll both be happier for it, and your business or personal life will improve as a consequence. Win-win.

Finally, at the heart of self-perspective is self-development, the inclination to self-improve, to develop the owner not the business, and to pursue meaningful objectives. These are the character attributes which exemplify a conscious entrepreneur.

Take a few minutes to sit and reflect. How would you rate yourself in these areas today?

2. Self-Expression

Self-expression entails skills fundamental to entrepreneurial success. Your ability to communicate effectively with other human beings—family, friends, employees, suppliers, associates, clients—has an enormous impact on your success.

And so self-expression, your ability to express what you're feeling in a verbal and non-verbal manner, is vital. As is treading the right side of the assertive/aggressive boundary.

Assertiveness enhances and opens communication, while aggressiveness detracts and shuts it down.

Finally, the self-expression component of emotional intelligence brings the ability to direct yourself, to be emotionally independent of others, and free from the need of direction, guidance and advice—typical character attributes found in highly successful entrepreneurs.

It's said great minds think alike. Unquestionably they do; however, great minds also think alone. Not to suggest great minds don't come together with other thinking partners because I can assure you, they do. In fact, it's a priority in their lives because they understand how vital the quality of their inner circle is to success.

Sadly, most business owners remain oblivious to this great truth, and it shows, in their results. The point is, great minds become great by thinking alone and often—by reflecting on any new input. Again, take a few minutes to reflect on the following questions:

- What score would you give yourself out of ten for your self-expression?
- How much do you enjoy time alone?
- How much time do you invest in reflecting and thinking inductively on your own?

3. Your People Skills

Where increased self-expression brings the ability to communicate more effectively with others, your people skills go much further. They bring the ability to connect.

How well do you form, maintain, and nurture mutually beneficial relationships?

Entrepreneurship calls for leadership. To their detriment, many entrepreneurs don't think of themselves as leaders, yet developing the owner not the business is a leadership activity—the most important of all: self-leadership.

> **"Coaching is the most transformational process known to mankind."**

For many years, I've had the privilege of working closely with leadership expert and prolific author, John. C. Maxwell. If you're not familiar with John, he was named the No. 1 leadership expert in the world by *Inc.* magazine in 2014. As well as collaborating together for many years, John has also influenced my life as a personal mentor.

At the heart of John's philosophy is one statement: leadership is influence, nothing more, nothing less. Emotional intelligence is ultimately about influence—influencing yourself and others to greater success. Or, to put it simply and succinctly, people skills.

For example, your ability to empathise, to understand another person's worldview and see the world through their eyes, is critical. You will never influence another person unless you understand their worldview. You don't have to agree with their point of view, you just need to respect and understand it so you can meet them where they are. There's a big difference between understanding a person and agreeing with them. Understanding another person's perspective of life is essential to influence. It's also imperative to coaching conversations.

Coaching is the most transformational process known to mankind. It's also the most misunderstood. What most people think is coaching, isn't.

Learning how to conduct powerful coaching conversations effectively with staff, clients and other major stakeholders isn't something most business owners would consider necessary to their success. They couldn't be more mistaken. Coaching is an essential skill for entrepreneurs—so crucial, in fact, I've trained and mentored thousands of entrepreneurs from all over the world in The Simpson Method of Transformational Coaching™ through my Conscious Coaching Academy™, and the Maxwell Method of Coaching I created in my collaboration with John C. Maxwell at the John Maxwell Team.

It isn't necessary for a business owner to be trained to the degree of a professional coach (although it would be enormously beneficial if he or she did). It is essential for any entrepreneur, though, to have the understanding and ability to hold coaching conversations.

This not only maximises the performance of staff or hired resources by compelling them to think inductively, becoming far more creative and self-sufficient as a consequence, it also enables the business owner to eventually remove himself from his business by creating a self-managing, self-multiplying enterprise.

Freedom is not a destination. It's not some distant utopia, forever sitting on the horizon. Freedom is a state of consciousness. You cannot experience freedom in the conditions and circumstances of your life without first experiencing it in your inner world—in your beliefs and the thinking they sponsor.

Entrepreneurial freedom only comes to those who empower others to think for themselves. It's why thousands of entrepreneurs have liberated their lives and created self-managing, self-multiplying businesses by equipping themselves through the world-class coaching trainings I've created.

And the value of developing your coaching ability doesn't end there. One of the most critical skills to master in entrepreneurial life is the ability to sell. To state the rather obvious, if no one is selling, no one is buying!

Selling isn't something you do *to* someone, it's something you do *for* them. Selling is influence. And coaching, next to how you conduct yourself in life, is the most potent form of influencing another person.

I only wish I'd been aware of coaching, and the power of it, during my seventeen-year corporate sales career. Most people think selling is about having the "gift of the gab". Not so.

The most important sales skills of all are listening deeply and asking powerful, curiosity-based, influential questions—two of the central tenets of coaching. I dread to think how much money I've left on the table over the years because I had no understanding of coaching or how to do it.

As we're on the topic of coaching, take time now to reflect on your people skills with the aid of the coaching questions below. As you do, be honest with yourself as you look in the metaphorical mirror these questions hold up to you. Remember: this isn't about judgement. We all have our shortcomings to overcome. This is about personal transformation.

- How do you rate yourself out of ten for your people skills?
- What examples can you think of where you influence people positively?
- What evidence do you have to demonstrate you value people?
- How much, and how deeply, do you listen to people?
- How curious are you about what's important to people, and what makes them tick?
- How many open, curiosity-based, inquisitive questions do you ask to understand others and their needs?
- How many one-to-ones do you hold, and how often, with key stakeholders in your business?
- If I were to observe you in a typical one-to-one interaction with a colleague or associate, what would I witness?
- Who's doing most of the talking in your one-

to-one interactions with staff, contractors, prospects, clients, or suppliers?

4. Decision-Making

This fourth component of emotional intelligence is covered at length in the final pillar of *The 4 Pillars of Mastery*™.

There's a science to making intelligent, effective decisions and I can assure you, the powerful strategies revealed in the final pillar will transform your life—and here's why.

Our lives proceed out of the choices and decisions we make—yet we're not educated at home, in academia, or in business, on how to make decisions effectively, which is absurd when you consider life demands we make hundreds of choices every day. So this aspect of emotional intelligence is your ability to make meaningful, timely, and relevant choices. This includes resisting impulsive and rash actions, and being able to view situations as they really are, rather than how you might fear or wish them to be.

There's nothing more dangerous in business than a self-deluded business owner. Believe me, I know, because I've been that business owner—and because of it, I paid the highest price an entrepreneur can pay when my business liquidated all those years ago.

- What rating, out of ten, would you give yourself for reality testing?
- What evidence supports your findings?
- Where have you made impulsive decisions recently? Think of as many examples as possible. In hindsight, what compelled you to make the decision so impulsively? What does this reveal

to you about your decision-making?

- What decisions have you procrastinated on or delayed far too long recently? Again, think of as many examples as possible. In hindsight, what caused you to hold back? What does this reveal to you about your decision-making?

- Finally, where have you made timely, well-thought-through decisions recently? What was the difference in these situations to those above, when your decisions were impulsive or delayed? How did you approach the decision-making process differently to allow you to make an effective decision quickly? What will prompt you to take the same approach whenever a decision is called for in future?

5. Stress Management

Finally, there's your ability to deal with stress. Stress can be a blessing or a curse. Too little of it and a compelling reason to change, grow, and improve is missing.

It's a recipe for disaster because as you appear to be coasting through life, life advances—so in effect, you're going backwards... and you won't even know it.

On the other side of the equation, too much stress is equally disastrous. In fact, it can kill. Aside from the life-detracting impact it has on your physical body, too much stress takes its toll on every other area of your life too. Sleeping patterns are disturbed, your ability to reason deteriorates, you're more prone to react than respond, and your ability to make decisions is significantly hampered. All of which plays havoc with your personal and professional relationships, your wellbeing, your finances, and your top and bottom line. The problem with stress is it's hard to monitor at a personal level. We're often the last to see how our behaviours have changed as a consequence of increased pressure.

Being open to what others are observing as you interact with them on a day-by-day basis is the most useful stress barometer of all. Give the people around you explicit permission to share with you any examples they feel demonstrate how your stress levels have become unhealthy.

We all need to look in the mirror more often, especially at times when the reflection isn't at its kindest. Of course, getting in the habit of regular self-diagnosis is the best solution of all.

Monitoring your inner world, particularly your emotions, and reflecting back and evaluating your thoughts, feelings, and actions in any past situation— without judgment—will create a powerful feedback mechanism to help you deal with stress far more effectively. Begin now.

How well do you manage the inevitable periods of increased stress in your life? How well do you remain poised and focused when facing changing, challenging, or unfamiliar conditions?

Consider these questions:

- How would you describe your ability to adopt a realistic yet optimistic positive attitude when facing adversity? These character traits are significant contributors to success.
- How would your inner circle describe you regarding your ability to handle stress and change?

Life Is A Big Psychological Game

I don't want to overcook the egg, but some eggs need overcooking: none of the attributes I've discussed above are taught in traditional or adult education.

Life is a game of psychology. Business is a game of psychology. Success is a game of psychology—and most people play poorly. You don't have to be one of them.

Taking the Entrepreneurial Wealth Scorecard™ is one of the most important things you'll ever do (remember, it's free to readers of this book—go to **christian-simpson.com/ult-score**). Reality testing— knowing where your current mental blueprint is taking you—is the first step in modifying your blueprint to create a more fulfilling, rewarding, and prosperous life. Only then can the creative powers of your psychology take you from where you are to wherever you intend to be. You can bet your bottom dollar—and believe me, it does come down to the bottom dollar for many people— any business owner lacking these skills is getting in their own way and dragging their business, and quality of life, down. The research and statistics speak for themselves.

Raising your consciousness, increasing your self-awareness, and becoming more emotionally and spiritually intelligent as a consequence makes more than good business sense—it's the smartest and most important thing you'll ever do. Make a habit of it, and I promise you, you'll live as very few people live.

You've now been exposed to a plethora of compelling and irrefutable research and evidence to support why developing the owner not the business is the ultimate entrepreneurial success strategy. It takes you from being the biggest liability in your business to its greatest asset.

When *that* shift happens, significant growth is inevitable, as this business owner can testify.

Nadeem's Story

I got stuck in the day-to-day activities working as a technician in my accountancy business. I wasn't seeing my business going anywhere, and I was stuck. I wanted to scale up and grow my business.

Then I found Christian's *4 Pillars of Mastery*™.

The First Pillar, which is all about developing the owner, not the business, has had a huge impact on my business—and equally on my personal life.

> **"There's no such thing as a highly successful solopreneur."**

Self-education is critical, and we can only grow our businesses if we overcome our limiting beliefs. That's exactly what the First Pillar taught me.

Only by developing myself using different tools by Christian, have I seen my business grow—and it's continuing to grow. I started on this First Pillar a year ago—and in just one year, my business has grown by 280%. And it's continuing to grow! The reason is I've learned how to grow myself first, so the business can grow with me. That 280% is a massive return on the investment I made with Christian. I've associated with growth-minded people, and I have seen this enhancement and growth in my business because of it.

Working through the Four Pillars has also had a profound effect on my personal life, which has improved immensely. I'm physically healthier and stronger than before. My relationships with my family, staff, and clients have also improved. And I can see my future in crystal clarity with the help of the tools provided by Christian.

Thinking Into Results: What Will Your Story Be?

Nadeem's success is no accident. He's put me, my explicit promise, my body of work, and the ultimate entrepreneurial success strategy to task—and transformed his business and personal results as a consequence. Nadeem's story contained many pearls of wisdom you'll be well served to pay close attention to.

However, when he made this passing comment: "That 280% is a huge return on the investment I made with Christian. I've associated with growth-minded people, and I have seen this enhancement and growth in my business because of it," Nadeem was revealing one of the most critical entrepreneurial success strategies of all time.

When it comes to success, no-one does it alone. There's no such thing as a highly successful "solopreneur", yet many business owners operate as if they're an island—even those surrounded by staff, colleagues and associates.

Running a business is often a lonely affair, not just at the start-up phase when there's literally no-one else, and all roads end with you, but also when you navigate the choppy waters of letting go of control to grow a team.

> "The most valuable environment you can put yourself in is the one where you're most uncomfortable."

Even then it's lonely. Nobody thinks like you. No-one understands you—not at the level you need to be understood. Even the most loyal, committed, enthusiastic team member won't get you, because they're not an entrepreneur, have never owned a business, and so can never truly understand the all-consuming emotional and spiritual attachment we entrepreneurs have to "our baby".

Entrepreneurial life is fraught with danger—none more so than the solo mentality. On the one hand, it's understandable: the very reason we're entrepreneurs is we're willing to get out there, take risks, and make it happen on our own. On the other hand, continuing to operate with a solo mentality will cripple your business.

And it goes beyond just building a team within your business. You need a team outside your business too. You need to be around people who understand the unique challenges associated with being a growth-oriented entrepreneur. People who can stretch you, and demonstrate in their own behaviour and by their individual results, they're the right people to be around. This is where the vast majority of business owners get it all wrong. Should the penny drop about the dangers of trying to do it alone, many people then make the grave error of following a well-trodden path to join traditional business networking groups.

There, they're surrounded by well-meaning, hard-working, average thinkers generating average results. They're not associating with people producing the kind of results they'd like to have, they're associating with people with people getting similar results (or worse) as they are! As the old axiom states: birds of a feather flock together. There's a reason why you don't find highly successful entrepreneurs in mainstream, traditional business networks. Those business owners who have risen out of the conformity of "normality"—beyond the struggle, mediocrity, underachievement, and "business as usual" of the masses—have, at some point, woken up to how the quality of people you associate with most— your inner circle—has an enormous influence on how successful, or not, you'll be.

Very few people wake up to this truth. Very few become aware of the importance of consciously choosing their inner circle. Consequently, their inner circle is created unconsciously, by default, and it tends to be people they're comfortable being around— people operating at the same level of consciousness and generating the same kind of results.

I promise you this: the most wanton waste of your time is time spent in environments not conducive to your growth. I also promise you this: the most valuable environment you can put yourself in is the one where you're most *uncomfortable*.

If you're the smartest person in the room, you're in trouble. If you're the "dumbest", or least successful, or both, and you're surrounded by people way above your "pay grade", you're onto a winner. In what way do the people in your inner circle set an example of growth? In what way are results in their personal and professional lives impressive? In what areas of life do they create results you'd like to emulate?

Which brings me neatly to the fact I'm not sharing any of this with some thinly disguised, ulterior motive to entice you to join one of my entrepreneurial groups.

These groups are strictly by invitation only. They simply wouldn't be anywhere near as transformational in their impact if they were open to every business owner. With good reason, they're not publicly available outside of my community of Conscious Entrepreneurs.

And anyway, this book may be the first time you and I have collaborated—in which case, it'll be premature. I'm not suggesting you can't join in the future, assuming you meet the strict qualifying criteria.

There is some good news, however, because by reading this far you've already demonstrated you're not a typical business owner. And so, if you've not done so already (and you'll be receiving regular communication from me if you have), I invite you to join my Conscious Entrepreneur community by taking the Entrepreneurial Wealth Scorecard™. The assessment and membership of this community is complimentary for business owners who've read this book. Go now to: **christian-simpson.com/ult-score**.

The most important thing to grasp is this: your inner circle should consist of people who support you unconditionally. They should be people who see more in you than you often see in yourself, who transform your thinking by challenging it with tough questions you'll never ask yourself, and who hold you accountable to your grandest ambitions and escalate you to new heights by elevating your consciousness.

In return, you must commit to doing the same for them.

Now we've established just how vital the quality of your inner circle is to your success, in Chapter 4 you'll hear from some of the most successful people in the world—and discover what they attribute to their success.

WARNING: Do not proceed to Chapter 4 yet!

Before you read on, make sure you download the free Success Implementation Guide™ (SIG) accompanying this book. The coaching resources within the SIG™ ensure the transformational benefits of the tried, tested, and proven strategies you've discovered so far are put to work in your business and professional life.

Should you proceed to Chapter 4 without engaging the questions in the SIG™, you will not internalise and grasp the powerful success principles of this chapter.

Do not make the grave error of convincing yourself you'll return to the resources later. Invariably, despite best intentions, it doesn't happen. I know, because I made the same mistake for many years—and it comes with a heavy price. Learn from my mistakes, apply yourself to the coaching questions immediately and, I can assure you, you'll reap the rewards.

christian-simpson.com/ult-sig

Scan me

Chapter 4

The Real Secret To Success

"If you want to change the fruits, you will first have to change the roots. If you want to change the visible, you must first change the invisible."

T. Harv Eker

Some years ago, in the USA, a survey of highly successful people was undertaken. Out of 1,001 participants, 733 were millionaires. Participants chose from a list of thirty factors which could have contributed to their success.

The top five responses were as follows:
1. Being honest with people.
2. Being well-disciplined.
3. Getting along with people.
4. Having a supportive spouse.
5. Working harder than most people.

I can't imagine any of these responses would come as a surprise to you. What's really interesting is all five reflect the character attributes of emotional and spiritual intelligence. None of them relates to intellectual prowess.

As Einstein put it: "Take care not to make the intellect our god; it has powerful muscles but no personality."

Having a high IQ was twenty-first on the list, endorsed by just twenty per cent of millionaires. Revealingly, the percentage dropped much lower when lawyers and physicians were removed from the analysis. Only thirty-two per cent of the millionaires in the survey were business owners.

"Your psychology determines everything."

My purpose in revealing this scientifically validated research with you is to, once more, reinforce the fundamental message of this book: developing your character, maturing the inherent, broader intelligences beyond your intellect, will determine your success in any given aspect of life.

Only then will your consciousness be raised; only then will your existing beliefs be modified; and only then will the quality of thinking you apply to your life improve. And only then will the results you create follow suit. Remember, your business and quality of life will never outgrow the quality of thinking you bring to them.

Ignore this truth at your peril, because the bottom line is if you fail to develop the owner rather than the business, you will fall short, by an enormous margin, of all you're capable of being. It's why this proven principle earns the right to be called the ultimate entrepreneurial success strategy.

Perhaps this was already self-evident to you. Maybe you already knew how vital self-discovery and self-development are to your success—you might even consider it obvious. Whether you knew it or not, whether it's obvious or not, isn't the issue. How much you engage in it, is.

My many years of experience and the plethora of research referenced throughout this book has led me to the same, undeniable conclusion: humans have an astonishing capacity to hear, read, and intellectually comprehend a message many times without truly grasping it. Given the state of our world at the hands of humanity, you don't need to look far for evidence to prove my point.

Throughout the ages, the greatest minds in every walk of life—people with very different perspectives, who've disagreed on almost every other subject—have unanimously agreed on one thing: what you and I think about, we ultimately become.

Your business and all it provides is only as good as the thinking you bring to it. If you're to become all you're capable of being as an entrepreneur, so you can enjoy the wealth, prosperity, and freedom making all the risk-taking, sacrifice, long hours, and blood, sweat and tears worthwhile, you just can't afford to ignore the ultimate cause and effect relationship in your life anymore.

Your psychology determines *everything*. Your current psychological blueprint brought you to where you are today... yet it can't take you any further. Which brings me to this—what I can promise you is the greatest news you'll ever receive in life as a human being, not just a business owner. It's the message I've been driving home throughout this book. It's an irrefutable truth most people find hard to swallow—because it comes with the ultimate responsibility.

Your psychology isn't fixed.

You can modify and improve it significantly and consistently—you just need to be shown how.

Make no mistake: in all your tomorrows, if you're to be, do, and have more in your life, you must not only grasp this truth, you have to put it to work and live into it. I'm showing you exactly how to do so in this book—not only by the words you're reading (they're just part of the equation and the least important of all) more so by the questions being asked of you.

Every question takes the quality of your thinking to new levels. Every question increases your self-awareness, raises your consciousness, and modifies your psychology so it can bring you the results you aspire to, rather than recreate the results you long to change. You won't be conscious of the impact most, if not all, the questions have, just as you're not aware of how an entire coastline changes when a stone is thrown from a beach—yet beneath the surface, it's never the same again.

When it comes to you and your marvellous mind, each question brings a modification destined to find its way into your results. It can't do anything else—the creative process, like life itself, is governed by natural law, and natural laws are unwavering in their expression.

I'm challenging you, and I'm testing your preconceived ideas about what matters most in entrepreneurial life. It's not about the business, it's about you—and if your life is to improve immeasurably, your

> **"If you ignore the ultimate entrepreneurial success strategy, you will liquidate untapped potential."**

priorities must change accordingly.

If you prioritise developing the business at the expense of developing yourself—which is exactly what most business owners do—if you follow the well-trodden path, focus exclusively on chasing the money, get distracted by the latest fads and shiny objects, prioritising the latest "ninja tactics" and focus on the "mechanics" of business rather than what's driving it—then mark my words: you will place enormous shackles on your ability, your business, your income, and your wealth—all while your health, relationships, and the rest of your life suffer. If you ignore the ultimate entrepreneurial success strategy, you will effectively liquidate your untapped potential. You will never become aware of the potential you're currently unconscious of, and it will never see the light of day in your results as a consequence. You'll fail to be all you're capable of being. I can't speak for you, but I can't think of anything worse than looking back in your later years on a life less lived. A life promising so much, yet never delivering what it could have delivered because the individual living it failed to develop the inner resources to make it happen.

And Now For Some More Great News...

The most imposing, impressive, and enduring architecture in the man-made landscapes of our world reveal a visible yet rarely thought-into secret: they all stand proud because of strong foundations.

No one, except expert civil engineers, gives a second thought to a building's foundations. They're hidden, out of sight, buried beneath all the eye can see—yet they're the most crucial part of the entire structure. Everything rises and falls on the strength of its foundations—a truth of such universal application it's genuinely astonishing we so often overlook it.

Naturally, the same principle applies to entrepreneurial success. The message in this first pillar of *The 4 Pillars of Mastery*™ is the all-important foundation for success. This is why it's the ultimate entrepreneurial success strategy: it determines everything.

Which brings us full-circle back to you and your potential. The answer to your problems, the solutions to your challenges, and the way to much greater success in your business and your personal life lies *within* you. Your inner world shapes your external reality. Success is an inside-out job. As is failure and everything in between. There is no escaping this truth, even if you choose to live in ignorance of it.

The creative process flowing to and through you never stops creating. The quality of its output is determined by the quality of consciousness being applied to it.

> **"The more aware you are, the more success you'll create."**

Struggle, failure and mediocrity—the day-to-day reality for most business owners—is a direct consequence of unconscious living. Ever-increasing success is a consequence of conscious living. The more aware you are, the more success you will create.

Tapping into the limitless potential within you isn't about acquiring knowledge outside yourself. The knowledge you seek already exists within you, you're just not conscious of it yet. Which is why you're not seeing the results you desire. It's why the term "untapped" is often used about potential.

Like an oil rig thrusting its drill into the Earth's crust to release the unseen, as you raise your consciousness, you'll become more aware of the potentiality you were previously unconscious of. As a consequence, you'll express more and more of your potential into your results. You'll never express what you're not aware of.

As you become more conscious in creating your outcomes, you'll be less controlled by the habitual thoughts and behaviours responsible for your existing conditions and circumstances. The quality of your thinking will improve, your actions will become more effective, and you'll attract much better results as a consequence. Moreover, you'll dramatically improve your intelligence. Yes, you did read that correctly, and yes, it's a bold statement—so I'll elaborate.

A few paragraphs ago I made an equally bold statement you can read and simultaneously pass over without grasping its implication. I pointed out how your psychology determines everything, how it's the architect of your existing results and, most importantly of all, it *isn't* fixed. Your psychology is pliable. You can continuously modify, and therefore improve, the psychological blueprint creating every result you call forth into your life experience.

To use a simple analogy, imagine owning a high-performance sports car equipped with an engine that, with the correct tools applied, had infinite potential. Yet to be compliant to existing and generally accepted performance "norms", ruling bodies insisted the manufacturer curtailed the car's capabilities, refusing to allow the limitless power of its engine to be advertised to the marketplace.

Consequently, the extraordinary power under the hood remained unknown to the vast majority of owners, only discovered and unleashed by those curious enough to get under the hood and work with the power.

This is exactly how most of us are programmed by the society humanity has constructed to remain ignorant of the astonishing and limitless power lying dormant within each and every one of us—a power forever seeking fuller expression through our natural gifts and abilities, limited only by our existing level of consciousness.

Extensive research into human intelligence revealed unlike IQ (which is fixed at birth, peaks at the age of seventeen, and deteriorates as we age) our emotional and spiritual intelligence can be increased throughout life.

Better still, your emotional and spiritual intelligence is innate. It's already within you, awaiting discovery through conscious recognition. It requires no development—you need developing, by raising your consciousness, to express more of it into your life.

You Do Not Know Your Power

This leads to the most eye-opening and empowering conclusion of our times: the intelligence having the greatest impact on our success is already within us in abundance.

In other words, the more you develop the owner, not the business... the more you deploy the ultimate entrepreneurial success strategy... the more self-discovery, self-improvement, and personal growth in your life... the more you'll bring equilibrium to the three psychological components of intelligence (IQ, EQ, SQ) within you... the more potential you'll express into your results… and the greater your success will be.

Here's what I can categorically guarantee: you do not know your power. You don't know a fraction of it. None of us do. The only difference between the small minority who enjoy outstanding success and those who don't is the appetite to do what needs to be done to release their inherent power. Which leads to an inevitable discussion about priorities. As I mentioned previously, success in life ultimately boils down to becoming conscious of habits no longer serving you and replacing them with behaviours that do.

Improving your emotional and spiritual intelligence isn't going to happen automatically. Just because we can express more of the intelligences within us having a far greater impact on our success than IQ, it doesn't mean we will. And just because greater expression of our intrinsic intelligences can be increased throughout life, it doesn't mean they will. Ageing, and the maturity of our emotional and spiritual intelligence, are not exclusive to each other. It doesn't happen without conscious intervention. You've got to play your part. You've got to be willing to put time, money, and your back into this. And given the evidence you've seen in this book about the impact it will have on your success in life, is there a more worthwhile activity to engage in? I don't think so. You couldn't have chosen a better time to open yourself up to this understanding. It's never been so imperative. And, in what some have labelled the "creative economy"—the age of the mind—it's never been so rewarding to have the psychological ability to think ability to think outside of convention, a point made at the very beginning of this book with Eric Hoffer's profound insight: "In times of change learners inherit the earth; while the learned find themselves beautifully equipped to deal with a world that no longer exists."

We've covered an enormous amount of ground in this book. I encourage you to take time to reflect on what you've read.

Don't forget, the most crucial step of all is addressing the all-important coaching questions at the end of each chapter—and in the Success Implementation Guide™ you can download at the end of each chapter. The same applies to every Pillar in the series. Which brings us nicely to yet another proven success strategy you can't afford to ignore...

Not All Activities Are Born Equal

In 1906, an Italian economist named Vilfredo Pareto noticed something remarkable: 80% of Italian land was owned by just 20% of the population. Intrigued, he looked for where else this trend might apply.

To his surprise, he found the same principle holds true in every other country he surveyed. Although his initial study focused on the distribution of wealth, it didn't remain exclusive to economics. For example, in his garden, Pareto observed 20% of the pea pods in his vegetable plot contained 80% of the peas.

Since then, a whole host of applications of what he named the 80/20 principle have been identified throughout life. The Pareto Principle, or 80/20 rule, is a well-established law of life today. It's not an exact science. The numbers are rarely precisely 80/20, and they don't have to add up to 100 either.

For example, back in 1992, a United Nations Development Program Report showed the uneven distribution of global income, with the wealthiest 20%

of the world's population controlling 82.7% of the world's income. The point is the principle itself, which states a relatively small number of causes have a vastly disproportionate influence on results. For example:

- 80% of your profits come from 20% of your products.
- 80% of your results come from 20% of your actions.
- You wear 20% of your clothes 80% of the time.
- 20% of your carpets get 80% of the wear.
- 80% of the work you do on any project happens in just 20% of the time you allocate to it (often the last 20% as the deadline looms).

> "Questions are the key to unlocking your untapped potential."

- 80% of your results in any area of your work occur in just 20% of the time you spend on them (which reveals the uncomfortable truth that 80% of our time is wasted).

Not only is this subject fascinating; it's also an invaluable insight for growth-orientated business owners like you and me. Understanding the 80/20 rule means we can dramatically increase our effectiveness and improve our profitability by prioritising activities bringing the highest returns.

Time is our most precious commodity. It's the only thing we inexorably spend and cannot earn. I can't give you more time, but I can bring you proven resources to ensure you use your time more effectively and profitability. Which is what you now have at your disposal with the ultimate entrepreneurial success strategy and *The 4 Pillars of Mastery*™.

Now for a familiar warning. This is only the beginning. The next step is the most vital of all, and the most tempting to skip. Skipping this step is a common error, and it has dire implications.

Believe me, I know because I was making this error for five years of my life—five years I'll never get back. This is why I created the Success Implementation Guide™ for each of *The 4 Pillars of Mastery*™.

As you now know only too well, your mind has been heavily programmed by years of academia to operate in a certain way. You've been trained to learn by memorising data and information so you can regurgitate it in the future.

Memorising the content in *The 4 Pillars of Mastery*™ isn't going to transform your life. You'll know a lot of great information, yet nothing much will change in your behaviours and results. Intellectual comprehension of the information within *The 4 Pillars of Mastery*™ is not difficult. It's not important, either.

What counts is putting these proven ideas to work. You have to apply wise concepts, and to apply them—in other words, to convert intellectual comprehension into behavioural output—you must first internalise them. The coaching questions in your Success Implementation Guide™ is how you do this.

The power is in the questions. Every question takes you within, beyond your intellect, to where your untapped potential resides, deep within your unconscious. The questions are the key to unlocking the door to your untapped potential. Remember, you can't express what you're not aware of.

The Ultimate 80/20 Activity Transforming Lives

The most accurate and insightful observation about what it takes to be successful in life came from the Swiss psychiatrist and psychoanalyst Carl Jung.

He said, "Until you make the unconscious conscious it will direct your life and you will call it fate."

Your existing results do not represent your potential—they merely represent your *current awareness* of your potential. Here's what a couple of decades and thousands of hours coaching thousands of people to much greater success has taught me: we are all unconscious to more potential within us than we can ever hope to express in a multitude of lifetimes.

It's the coaching questions in your Success Implementation Guide™, not the words on these pages, that make the unconscious conscious. I cannot overemphasise how important this is. Do not fall for the compelling temptation to skip applying yourself to the coaching questions I've prepared for you. Beware. In other words, *be aware*. There is something within you seeking to limit you. It's the belief system responsible for the current conditions and circumstances of your life. Your current belief system is the architect of your current psychological blueprint.

Its priority is to keep you "safe" by maintaining the status quo in your life. Your belief system will attempt to sabotage any process representing growth—including this one—because it recognises this as a process of transformation, and transformation means the end of the belief system in its current form. This limiting belief knows how to "play you" more than you can imagine.

The hardest work is to recognise a limiting belief, which is why I'm preparing you with these words.

Your limiting belief will push self-sabotaging thoughts into your mind. It's done it many times before and it has succeeded in its objective. Every time you've failed to make an aspiration a reality in your life, your existing belief system is the culprit subtly sabotaging your success.

Your limiting belief sows subtle seeds of doubt, feeding scepticism. It promotes the idea you're "too busy" to answer questions, or "you've got better things to do" or "you haven't got time". Don't give in to the temptation. Success and the awakening preceding it comes at a price. Even the most highly conscious individuals battle with the devil within—one famously did so for forty days and forty nights. The coaching questions are the answer you've been looking for—they and they alone are the true force of transformation in this body of work. Read Rob's story, and see for yourself.

Rob's Story

I run multiple operations, which I don't work in personally—and a training academy, which I do work in. I developed the training academy to educate, upskill, and develop personally the managers and staff of the pubs I run as businesses.

I'm about to add two more establishments to double my capacity and trading volumes—and all this happened within 12 months of association with Christian.

I've always advocated growth and self-development and studied neurolinguistic psychology to Masters level. Then, for ten years, I lost my way. I didn't do any further personal development. Until I discovered *The 4*

Pillars of Mastery™.

I related to the Four Pillars massively and realised—yes—I need to develop further if I wanted my business to develop. After I worked through the First Pillar, I heightened my self-awareness. It made me look at where I was as a business person—and I realised, "No, I've been associating with the wrong people and the wrong ideas, and if I want to develop myself and my business I need to do more."

The Four Pillars is responsible for the mind-shift in thinking about success. People won't come to you just because you have a portfolio of businesses. Business won't just come to you. You have to make it happen yourself.

The Four Pillars gave me clarity, too. They gave me a new pathway to run on, and a new association of business persons who are already successful in their own right. They were able to transfer some of their knowledge base to me, so I've grown massively. The biggest feature of the Four Pillars, for me, has to be "develop the owner, not the business". Everything I do now is based on that.

When I found the Four Pillars, I had two establishments turning over £1.4 million. I'm about to add another three businesses, and my turnover is now £4.3 million—just from improving my understanding and awareness of what I need to do to grow. After the Four Pillars, I quickly joined Christian's Elite Mastermind™—by the time I'd gone through twelve months of the Mastermind, I'd taken my turnover from £1.7 million to around £4.3 million. In the next twelve months, I will smash through a £10 million turnover—and those businesses will return me a minimum of 10% profit.

I challenge anyone else to deliver the same standard of performance in what will have been two years. It's all down to the Mastermind and starting with the Four Pillars. It's all down to developing yourself because the businesses will sort themselves out as you do so. The focus is there for me because I'm challenged on accountability at meetings, summits, one-to-ones, and it all started with the springboard of the Four Pillars. Then *The 7 Steps to Success*™.

The real game changer was when I read you are a byproduct of your actions and behaviours. The results you've achieved to date—you're responsible for those results. If you want greater results, you need to change your mindset.

Change your mindset and, consciously and unconsciously, you'll change your behaviours and actions. And you'll see a change in your results. But that's not all. It's not just business that's improved for me. I am more self-aware as an individual. I had a lot of historical issues from bullying and abuse at school—I was badly beaten and hospitalised. And my dad had severe mental health issues. Watching him taken away in a straitjacket affected me badly. I had a lot of negative energy which expressed itself in aggression—I took any challenge as an aggressive challenge, and my reactions were often physical. This didn't bode well for me as an employer or a person. I wanted to increase my staff, and I couldn't have volatility in my life. It would end in trouble, and I didn't want to hurt anyone.

Christian and my Elite Mastermind™ Group Leader, Paull Newsome, encouraged me to go and seek psychological help, and I did. I've had twelve appointments in four months. Before I did, I was hypertensive with dangerously high blood pressure—it generally hovered around 160/120. Since having my treatments, I've been able to stop taking my medication, and my blood pressure has come down to 120/70. Christian and his team didn't "fix" me, but without his Four Pillars, the Elite Mastermind™, and his team, I don't know if I'd have asked for help. Christian recognised I had a serious problem and encouraged me to get professional help. My wife and friends cannot believe the difference in me. Running and developing a business and staff is stressful in itself, but I'm more relaxed than I have ever been before.

I've found a different, better, way of doing and living business. I was in a quagmire of mediocrity and pain, and Christian and the Four Pillars have helped me change my life for the benefit of everyone I associate with. Today I am truly flying with eagles, not scratching with turkeys.

Thinking Into Results: What Will Your Story Be?

Rob and his story are truly inspiring. Like the thousands of entrepreneurs who've come to *The 4 Pillars of Mastery*™, he is living proof you can transform your life if you're just willing to transform what creates your life.

To steal mercilessly from the wisdom of the T. Harv Eker quote at the start of this chapter, if you want to change the fruits, you have to change the roots.

WARNING: Do not proceed to Chapter 5 yet!

Before you read on, make sure you download the free Success Implementation Guide™ (SIG) accompanying this book. The coaching resources within the SIG™ ensure the transformational benefits of the tried, tested, and proven strategies you've discovered so far are put to work in your business and professional life.

Should you proceed to Chapter 5 without engaging the questions in the SIG™, you will not internalise and grasp the powerful success principles of this chapter.

Do not make the grave error of convincing yourself you'll return to the resources later. Invariably, despite best intentions, it doesn't happen. I know, because I made the same mistake for many years—and it comes with a heavy price. Learn from my mistakes, apply yourself to the coaching questions immediately and, I can assure you, you'll reap the rewards.

christian-simpson.com/ult-sig

Chapter 5

Your Success Implementation Guide™

"When we have arrived at the question, the answer is already near."

Ralph Waldo Emerson

The *Four Pillars of Mastery*™ is a process, not a single event. Transformation doesn't come from a singularity, it comes from a process, and invariably people overestimate the power of events and underestimate the power of processes.

Frequency and regularity are essential components in transformation, so I encourage you to return to the First Pillar once you've worked through the entire series.

Joe Mairura is a business owner who's been in my community of Conscious Entrepreneurs for some years, so he knows *The 4 Pillars of Mastery*™ very well. Here's his take on how you get the most out of the opportunity before you: "It's not something you can go through just once, because every time you go through [the Four

Pillars], you see something different. You begin to look at things entirely differently from the way you first do when you first discover them.

"I listen to the Four Pillars once every three or four months. Every time I hear it, I pick up something new or see something completely different. It's a resource for life, not a one-off. That's the wonderful thing about it."

> **"Frequency and regularity are essential components in transformation."**

Remember: the content never changes—you do. Every time you come back to these pages and, crucially, the transformational questions in your Success Implementation Guide™, your consciousness is raised. You'll pick up on ideas you didn't absorb first time— because your awareness wasn't where it needed to be to receive them.

The Ancient Greeks understood this principle of life. It's why they said repetition is the mother of all learning.

You are now in the unlearning process. Pillar 1's purpose is to continually reframe your perspective about yourself, your potential, your business, and the possibilities in your future. Now it's time to let the questions do their work.

The second Pillar of *The 4 Pillars of Mastery*™ series brings you a detailed understanding of the creative process flowing to and through you.

If you're to master anything, you must first understand it—how it operates, the rules of the game, whether the game's in the boardroom, on the sports field—or what determines success in every game in life, the innermost workings of your mind.

The same principle applies to life. To master life, and enjoy the fruits of whatever extraordinary entrepreneurial success and an outstanding life represent to you, you must be willing to go within and master yourself.

All mastery begins with clarity, and much greater clarity will come to you every time you return to this book. And the trend will continue throughout every step of *The 4 Pillars of Mastery*™ resources, and what lies beyond them.

For now, it's time to engage your mind in a way it's rarely, if ever, been engaged before so you can ignite the infinite power awaiting conscious recognition within you.

As Thomas Troward put it so perfectly in *The Spirit Of Opulence*: "Where we are drawing from the infinite we need never be afraid of taking more than our share." As you move through the self-discovery process within the *The 4 Pillars of Mastery*™, you'll soon gain an appreciation of how your inner resources are truly infinite by nature.

Enjoy the process of becoming more.

Next Steps

"Men are anxious to improve circumstances, but never willing to improve themselves; they therefore remain bound."

James Allen

Allow me to be the first to congratulate you. In picking up this book, you're in a small minority. In reading it, you're in an even smaller minority. And, if you've applied yourself with rigorous honesty to the all-important coaching questions in the Success Implementation Guide™, you're truly in rarified air.

That in itself bodes well for your future. If you continue to adopt the behaviours of the Top 0.1%, if you continue to develop the owner not the business, making the ultimate entrepreneurial success strategy a priority in your life, it's only a matter of time until your results follow. It's a lawful process.

To state what is now rather obvious, Pillar 1 is the first of four. There's still so much more to reveal to you, so here's a brief synopsis of what's coming your way. Remember: things have to change in you for things to change for you.

Pillar 2: Influencing at Cause, Not Effect

As you've discovered in this book, just 0.1% of business owners are millionaires. The vast majority wallow in struggle, underachievement, and mediocrity totally unnecessarily—all because they live their lives completely ignorant of the creative process flowing to and through them. As you now know, your existing results, conditions, and circumstances are effects. They have ancestry. If you're to bring significant, continuous, and lasting improvements to your life and business, you must understand the ancestry and cause of those effects so you can consciously influence the outcome. The second Pillar in the series builds on the ultimate entrepreneurial success strategy of the first Pillar, revealing all you need to take control and master the creative process within you.

Pillar 3: Focus on Potential, Not Performance

Just a single shift in your perception can transform your life for the better. Most business owners fail to accomplish their entrepreneurial dreams because of a preoccupation with current results. They focus on what they want to change rather than results they'd like to experience.

Think about it: if you put as much focus, time, effort, and energy into your potential as you do your performance, what do you think the implication would be for the growth of your business? Your perception and focus will shift forever because of what you'll discover in Pillar 3 of *The 4 Pillars of Mastery*™.

Pillar 4: Decision Making— Know the Why Not the How

Earlier I shared how the teaching in this Pillar alone will improve your life immeasurably. You're about to have your understanding of effective decision-making turned on its head. Highly successful entrepreneurs make decisions in an entirely different way to the underachieving masses.

The quality of your decisions determines the quality of your life. Decision-making is an essential skill for a successful life, yet when were you taught how to make qualitative decisions quickly and effectively?

There's a science to intelligent, effective decision-making, and most people will never know it. Once you've discovered the powerful information and strategies waiting for you in Pillar 4, you'll be among the few who not only know it, you'll also understand it—so you can instantly put it to good use to dramatically accelerate your success.

Beyond The 4 Pillars of Mastery™

Thank you for investing your time in this book. As a fellow entrepreneur, I fully appreciate the value of time, so your commitment to reading this work is not lost on me.

If you feel like you've been drinking from a fire hose, I understand. I encourage you to reframe your thinking because while there are no quick fixes, easy answers, or magic formulas to outstanding entrepreneurial success, there are proven methods and shortcuts. If you're feeling disturbed or out of sorts in some way, have no concern. It's a perfectly natural response. Exposure to these ideas, challenges, preconceptions, beliefs, and assumptions can take some getting used to. Despite how it may feel initially, I can assure you it's a fantastic place to be.

This is only the beginning. You never graduate from self-improvement because growth, for a truly successful individual, never ends. There's always more.

I'm a realist. I've been in this business for a long time. As this book has focused exclusively on the Top 0.1%, it's important to highlight the correlation between how most people will approach this book, and the statistics and percentages of entrepreneurial life.

Most people who find this book will either never read it, or only partially read it. A much smaller minority will read it... but they'll *only* read it. They won't take action and use the coaching resources in each chapter and in the Success Implementation Guide™, so the principles and strategies can't do what they've been proven to do over and over again. Consequently very little, if anything, will change and the business owner concerned will continue to recreate their struggle, mediocrity, and underachievement unnecessarily.

For years this frustrated me because I knew what these ideas had done for me and the thousands of people who've embraced and engaged them (although my frustrations paled into insignificance compared to those who ignored these methods and continued to work harder for longer only to suffer ever-diminishing returns).

Today, experience has given me the wisdom to no longer be attached to the outcome. I rest my head on my pillow, safe in the knowledge I've done all I can to equip those who come to this book with the means to make freedom, wealth, and prosperity in all areas of life a reality.

My sincerest hope is you'll be one of the minority who will take action. As the German philosopher Goethe said: "Before you can do something, you must first be something". To be in the Top 0.1%, you need to do as the Top 0.1% do—and it begins here, right now, with the proven principles at your disposal.

Your first step is to put the ultimate entrepreneurial success strategy to work by developing the owner, not the business. Without greater awareness of who you are, who you choose to be, and the limiting beliefs getting in your way, the success you aspire to and are capable of will elude you forever. By the time you've applied yourself across the entire *4 Pillars of Mastery*™, you'll have transformed your inner world with the proven resources, tools, and strategies at your disposal.

By natural law, as you've seen from a plethora of examples in this First Pillar, transformation in your outer world will follow. To once again draw from the wisdom of the Victorian author James Allen:

"You cannot travel within and stand still without."

As with any journey taking you from one place to another, the most critical step is the first.

And the first step on any journey has to be establishing where you are, which leads me to...

The Entrepreneurial Wealth Scorecard™

The Entrepreneurial Wealth Scorecard™ is so vital for you because it's the world's leading assessment of wealth-generating ability for entrepreneurs and business owners. It's been purposefully designed to be simple and easy to take. I've mentioned it a few times during Pillar 1, and because it's such an essential step in the process, it deserves further explanation here. As it stands today, is your existing psychology engineered to generate significant success, wealth, and freedom in your life?

Or are you currently mentally engineered to recreate your existing norms—the very results you must want to change to have picked this book up in the first place?

Through a series of simple, easy-to-complete self-assessment criteria, this potent resource provides you with an accurate and revealing insight into your current psychological blueprint and where it's likely to take you, should you leave it unchanged.

The eight criteria are as follows:
1. Authentically Ambitious
2. Total Responsibility
3. The Coachable Unlearner
4. The Long-Term Thinking
5. The Tenacious Disciplinarian
6. The Risk Taker
7. The Change Embracer
8. The Go-Getting, Go-Giver

How you respond to each section will place you within one of four categories:
1. Scarcity/Poverty Consciousness

2. Aspiring Mass Consciousness
3. Unconscious Stagnation
4. Conscious Entrepreneur

Once your answers have been reviewed, you'll receive an email containing your result and a full description of your particular group.

Remember, your existing psychological blueprint does not define you. You are not your programming, and you can modify your mindset to create the results you want—rather than the results you want to change.

You can take the Entrepreneurial Wealth Scorecard™—and join my community of Conscious Entrepreneurs—by going to the web address below:

christian-simpson.com/ult-score

Further Entrepreneurial Success Resources From Christian Simpson

CONSCIOUS ENTREPRENEUR INNER CIRCLES

The Conscious Entrepreneur Community

The Conscious Entrepreneur Community is Christian's globally renowned inner circle of growth-orientated, success-driven entrepreneurs.

Members receive Christian's infamous thought-provoking emails, in which he shares major personal and entrepreneurial lessons of past and present, packed with a potent mix of mind-expanding insight, eye-opening yet challenging truths and, as you might expect, a good dose of humour and non-conformist perspectives.

The Conscious Entrepreneur Community is where members get complimentary access to powerful and proven resources, free telephone seminars and webinars, as well as exclusive access to Christian's transformation entrepreneurial success programmes, products and services not available to the general public. Membership of the Conscious Entrepreneur Community is complimentary to growth-minded business owners and entrepreneurs who are genuinely committed to enjoying a level of personal and professional success most people will never know. To join this thriving and growing community, you must first take the Entrepreneurial Wealth Scorecard™ by visiting:

christian-simpson.com/ult-score

Entrepreneurial Mastery Inner Circle™

As you've discovered in this book, your success will be determined, to an enormous degree, by the quality of your environment and the quality of the people around you. The dumbest approach to entrepreneurial life is trying to do it alone. There is no such thing as a highly successful solopreneur. No-one does it alone. The second-dumbest approach to entrepreneurial life is to join traditional business networks filled with well-meaning, average thinking, underachieving business owners. Birds of a feather flock together, and there's an excellent reason why highly successful entrepreneurs are not found in traditional business networks. It doesn't end there.

If you're going to be increasingly successful in life, you need access to expertise. The top performers in every walk of life have a coach by their side to ensure they're at the peak of their powers. They also have mentors to draw wisdom, guidance and experience from.

It can take years to get the right calibre of inner circle. And it takes a very healthy six figures to gain access to world-class coaches and mentors.

That's why Christian Simpson created the Entrepreneurial Mastery Inner Circle™, a community of like-minded, growth-oriented, success-driven, more conscious entrepreneurs who not only have the opportunity to interact with a diverse, supportive network of upwardly mobile business owners, they get direct access to world-class coaching—plus mentoring from highly successful entrepreneurs.

The Entrepreneurial Mastery Inner Circle™ is unprecedented and unrivalled in the extraordinary value it brings. Membership is by invitation only, exclusive to members of Christian's Conscious Entrepreneur community. To join the Conscious Entrepreneur community, take the Entrepreneurial Wealth Scorecard™ via the URL below.

christian-simpson.com/ult-score

The Elite Mastermind™

Back in the early part of the twentieth century, Andrew Carnegie, a billionaire and the world's richest man at the time, met a young journalist called Napoleon Hill. Carnegie, a steel baron, credited his entire fortune to the mastermind process. All his employees were in a mastermind and, given Carnegie had sixty millionaires in his employ, all created by the mastermind process, he was worth paying attention to.

Napoleon Hill, on Carnegie's sponsorship, went on to interview the most successful people of his generation, and later published his findings in his books *The Laws*

145

of Success and *Think & Grow Rich*.

In both, Hill discussed the power of the mastermind process, and how the most powerful and successful people, without exception, were members of a mastermind group. Today, highly successful entrepreneurs gather in masterminds—a small group of carefully chosen thinking partners to build a lifetime of mutual success with.

Christian Simpson built The Elite Mastermind™ process on the Carnegie and Hill philosophy. Then he enhanced it further by adding powerful elements such as one-to-one coaching, accountability meetings and private membership groups. It all began some years ago with Christian's own Elite Mastermind™, a group of very successful entrepreneurs who still gather regularly and collaborate in the Elite Mastermind™ process. They're also mentors to the Conscious Entrepreneurs in the Entrepreneurial Mastery Inner Circle™.

Today, Elite Mastermind™ groups are transforming the lives of business owners in Europe and the Americas.

Applications to join an Elite Mastermind™ are strictly by invitation only, and exclusive to members of Christian's Conscious Entrepreneur community.

There's a thorough due diligence process for all applications, and members must meet specific qualifying criteria. Far more applications are declined than accepted, and there's a healthy waiting list to join.

To become a member of the Conscious Entrepreneur Community (it's free), take The Entrepreneurial Wealth Scorecard™ via the URL below.

christian-simpson.com/ult-score

ONLINE RESOURCES

The 4 Pillars of Mastery™

At the time of writing the first edition of this book, The 4 Pillars of Mastery™ resources have transformed the personal and professional lives of business owners and entrepreneurs in 161 countries. The 4 Pillars of Mastery™ reveal transformational strategies to increase self-awareness, raise consciousness, and evoke the psychology of success and wealth generation in entrepreneurs.

Through a series of ground-breaking video tutorials and world-class coaching resources in the accompanying Success Implementation Guide™, The 4 Pillars of Mastery™ will put you on a trajectory to a level of entrepreneurial success most business owners will never know—the kind enjoyed by the Top 0.1%. The 4 Pillars of Mastery™ is exclusive to members of Christian's Conscious Entrepreneur Community. To join, take the Entrepreneurial Wealth Scorecard™ via the URL below.

christian-simpson.com/ult-score

The 7 Steps to Success™

The 7 Steps to Success™ has been described by users as a comprehensive blueprint for extraordinary entrepreneurial success. It answers the biggest questions in entrepreneurial life—from tools to accurately diagnose reality, to defining purpose, creating a compelling personal and professional vision, to a life-changing insight into the laws of goal achieving, ensuring success in every goal you set—all broken down into simple, easy-to-apply steps you can put to work in your business and personal life straight away.

Containing more than two-and-a-half hours of leading-edge strategies, this powerful and proven system of video tutorials and coaching resources is a natural progression from The 4 Pillars of Mastery™.

And, as with all Christian Simpson's globally acclaimed body of work, The 7 Steps to Success™ will continue to take you, your business, and your quality of life to the next level, regardless of the level of success you already enjoy. It's an investment for life, and returning to the programme over and over again will continue to accelerate your growth and success for the rest of your days.

The 7 Steps to Success™ is only available to members of Christian's Conscious Entrepreneur community.

To join, take The Entrepreneurial Wealth Scorecard™ via the URL below:

christian-simpson.com/ult-score

Science of Success 1

There is a science to success, it's just most people never discover what it is. Christian's Science of Success (SOS) is a suite of powerful and proven entrepreneurial success experiences—from extensive online educational experiences to live, in person seminars—all packed with tried, tested, and proven transformational strategies.

Even though each component of the SOS system is independent, together they crystallise Christian's core philosophy of developing the psychology of wealth generation first, before discovering the astonishingly profitable and proven marketing strategies to make wealth, prosperity, and freedom a reality in a business owner's life.

It begins with Christian's flagship self-transformation experience, Science of Success 1. Here you'll be exposed to the most transformational personal growth journey of your life. Through a series of eye-opening and mind-expanding webinars, Christian will guide you through the life-changing strategies he discovered directly from some of the greatest thinkers in personal success—proven principles passed down through generations—methods Christian uses to transform every aspect of his life for the better... and which continue to powerfully impact the lives of thousands of people around the globe.

Science of Success is exclusive to members of Christian's Conscious Entrepreneur Community. To join, take the Entrepreneurial Wealth Scorecard™ via the URL below.

christian-simpson.com/ult-score

Science of Success 2

Science of Success 2 is an entirely different proposition. Where Science of Success 1 focused exclusively on developing the psychology of success and wealth generation, Science of Success 2 shares the leading-edge, astonishingly profitable direct response marketing strategies to make the wealth, prosperity and freedom of the entrepreneurial dream a reality.

These proven methods are unknown to most business owners. They were to Christian when his first business failed in 2009. The indignity of this experience compelled Christian to find and hire entrepreneurs who'd proven, by their results, they knew how to build highly profitable, multi-million dollar enterprises.

By deploying what he discovered, Christian's business grew from zero to a million plus in less than four years.

Very few business owners understand there are two kinds of marketing in business, only one of which works for small businesses. Sadly, the vast majority are wasting untold amounts of time pouring hard-earned money down the drain on marketing initiatives which only work for large, household brands.

If cash flow is the lifeblood of an enterprise, marketing is its heartbeat. It doesn't matter how good you are at what you do. It doesn't matter how good your product or service is. And it doesn't matter how good at selling you are. If you don't have anyone to sell to, if you don't have anyone to provide your product or service to, the rest is academic.

If you don't have an effective and profitable marketing engine, with multiple online and offline channels feeding your business—your business, your income, and your entire quality of life are in a very precarious and vulnerable position.

Science of Success 2 is exclusive to members of Christian's Conscious Entrepreneur Community. To join, take the world's leading assessment of wealth generating ability, the Entrepreneurial Wealth Scorecard™—access is complimentary via the URL below.

christian-simpson.com/ult-score

LIVE SEMINAR & WORKSHOP EXPERIENCES

Entrepreneurial Elite Think Tank™

Entrepreneurial Elite Think Tank™ is a live event like no other. Christian is a veteran of seminars. He's travelled the world to attend workshops, seminars and events to improve himself, and he still does today.

As valuable as seminars unquestionably are, though, the one-way information dump, the same flawed "learning" model on which the traditional education system is built, left a gaping need unaddressed in the market. Christian saw that need—particularly for business owners and entrepreneurs (because he is one!)—and created a powerful solution. Launched in the US in 2013, Entrepreneurial Think Tank™ is a uniquely powerful, highly interactive, in-person event where you get to join a group of like-minded entrepreneurs in a live, in-person experience with Christian.

What makes Entrepreneurial Think Tank™ different is it's all about you: your business, your goals, dreams and ambitions and, more specifically, the challenges getting in the way. Not only will you be able to interact directly with Christian and dramatically accelerate your success by benefiting from his world-renowned coaching expertise; you'll also experience a plethora of breakthroughs from observational learning—listening to and witnessing the interaction between Christian and other business owners.

After all, we all have different businesses, different backgrounds, different cultures, different perspectives, and different maps of the world—but the challenges we

151

face are universal.

In 2015, Christian took this powerful concept further by creating Entrepreneurial Elite Think Tank™, in which he's joined at the front of the room by a panel of successful entrepreneurs drawn from his own inner circle, his own Elite Mastermind™ group, and his Conscious Entrepreneur Community, so business owners in the audience can draw from their experience and wisdom.

Entrepreneurial Elite Think Tank™ events are open to the public, and places sell out fast. Priority access is given to members of Christian's Conscious Entrepreneur Community. To join, take the Entrepreneurial Wealth Scorecard™ via the URL below.

christian-simpson.com/ult-score

Science of Success—LIVE!

Unquestionably one of the most transformational live experiences on the planet, Science of Success— LIVE! is a two-day in-person immersion in life mastery—revealing the most powerful personal success strategies known to mankind.

Christian and his team expertly guide you through an eye-opening and life-changing experience, ensuring you leave this event an entirely different proposition to the world than when you arrived. Science of Success—LIVE! is exclusive to members of Christian's Conscious Entrepreneur Community. To join, take the Entrepreneurial Wealth Scorecard™ via the URL below.

christian-simpson.com/ult-score

Zero to A Million™: How Today's Top 0.1% Create Wealth, Prosperity & Freedom

The title says it all. This powerful seminar, which leads into Science of Success 2, gives participants a comprehensive insight into how Christian took his startup from zero to a million in less than four years.

Revealing a level of marketing intelligence used by the Top 0.1% to create lucrative online and offline sales funnels, with premier positioning and pricing, participants are immersed in the specifics of how the wealthy minority go about building businesses in an entirely different way to how most people believe a small business is built.

It's a career and life-defining experience, and exclusive to members of the Conscious Entrepreneur Community.

To join, take the Entrepreneurial Wealth Scorecard™ via the URL below.

christian-simpson.com/ult-score

The 8 Fundamentals of Entrepreneurial Wealth & Freedom™

Order, structure, and clarity are essential for success. Until now, no-one equipped business owners and entrepreneurs with a detailed blueprint providing the definitive step-by-step roadmap to make the wealth and freedom of the entrepreneurial dream a reality.

Drawn from his close collaborations with highly successful entrepreneurs from across the globe,

Christian Simpson shares every single step a business owner must take to successfully navigate the inevitable ceilings of complexity arising from the perpetual growth of self-managing, self-multiplying enterprises.

You'll discover why self-education, direct response marketing, financial education, coaching for performance, self-removal, and other vital topics are fundamental to your growth and success.

christian-simpson.com/ult-score

The Conscious Coaching Academy™

You may not realise it, but one of the most essential skills for an entrepreneur is the ability to coach.

Coaching is the most powerful, transformational process known to mankind. Nothing compares to coaching in terms of influencing another human being to much higher levels of performance in all aspects of life.

Your ability to remove yourself from your business, by either keeping it as a profit centre when you move on to the next project, or selling it with an extra zero on the asking price for a life-changing payday, depends on you equipping your business with a leadership team capable of running and growing it without your involvement. Either way, your ability to coach others is vital to your success.

Christian Simpson is a globally acclaimed master in the coaching industry. He's not only recognised as a world-class practitioner in coaching, and the world's leading coach and mentor to entrepreneurs and business owners, he's also known as the leading trainer of professional coaches in the world. He's the creator of

The Simpson Method of Transformational Coaching™ and The Maxwell Method of Coaching (part of his collaboration with world leadership expert, John C. Maxwell).

To date, Christian has trained over 30,000 people from every corner of the globe to the highest standards in the coaching profession.

Christian's Conscious Coaching Academy™ (CCA) provides multiple levels of coaching training to aspiring and established professional coaches, from the basics of certification to higher level accreditations. Not only that, CCA equips professional coaches with the tools, resources, and skills to become outstandingly successful entrepreneurs.

The CCA also provides entrepreneurs and business owners with certification level training in essential influencing skills to make self-removal and freedom a reality in their lives. By discovering how to conduct powerful coaching conversations with key employees, collaborators and colleagues, the business owner creates a self-sufficient leadership team to ensure the business becomes a self-managing, self-multiplying enterprise.

The Conscious Coaching Academy™ is exclusive to either the Conscious Coach™ or the Conscious Entrepreneur Communities. You can join the latter by taking The Entrepreneurial Wealth Scorecard™ (it's complimentary to business owners) via the URL below.

christian-simpson.com/ult-score

Made in the USA
Middletown, DE
03 November 2020